Cloth Dolls
for Textile Artists

Cloth Dolls
for Textile Artists

Ray Slater

INTERWEAVE PRESS.
interweavebooks.com

For
Mum and Dad
and
Tim, Rosie and Thomas

With thanks to Vivienne Rudd, friend and guinea-pig, and Pat Lumsdale for helpful advice. A special thank-you to June Evans, friend and nimble-fingered word wizard. Also thanks to Alan Lambert for the occasional use of his front lobe.

First published in the United States by
Interweave Press, LLC
201 East Fourth Street
Loveland, CO 80537-4632
interweavebooks.com

Copyright © Batsford 2008
Text © Ray Slater 2008

Library of Congress Cataloging-in-Publication Data

Slater, Ray.
  Cloth dolls for textile artists / Ray Slater, author.
    p. cm.
  Includes index.
  ISBN 978-1-59668-087-6 (hardcover)
  1. Dollmaking. 2. Cloth dolls. I. Title.
  TT175.S556 2008
  745.592'21--dc22

                                              2008005373

10 9 8 7 6 5 4 3 2 1

Reproduction by Dot Gradations Ltd, UK
Printed by Craft Print Ltd, Singapore

Page 1: This doll's headdress was created using crossway waves (see page 51).

Page 2: Three wired dolls. These are created around a wire armature for maximum flexibility (see chapter 2).

Below and opposite: This doll's headdress was created using the cutwork technique (see page 115). The same fabric was used to create a dainty shoe (opposite page).

Contents

Introduction

In simple terms, a cloth doll is a figurative soft sculpture, but it is the interpretation of an idea and the combination of raw materials that enables these unique and inspirational figures to come to life.

Cloth dolls and figures appeal to artists from many different backgrounds and this has led to the cross-fertilization of different media and styles. Realism and abstraction, fantasy and fine art are often combined with hand- and machine-made textiles, printed and painted fabrics, to create wonderful figurative works of art.

The inspiration for soft dolls and figures can come from many diverse sources including paintings, sculptures, fashion, magazines, costume or fairy and folk tales, as well as from observation of our fellow creatures. If you keep an open mind, you need never be short of ideas.

You may find it helpful to create your own source information book, in which you can keep anything that may inspire you, to be explored and developed at a later stage.

This book introduces you to some basic doll techniques. It also includes textile techniques for creating fabrics, that can be used either for making the actual doll or for costume.

The *Stump Doll* produced from simple shapes provides the perfect vehicle for this type of textile fabric.

The *Wired Armature Doll* can be arranged in different poses to create a sense of fluidity. Here, hand stitching and *bias rouleau* are used to create surface detail and texture.

The *Stuffed Cloth Doll* is brought to life by the use of transfer-dyed fabric embellished with free-machine embroidery and motifs created with a soldering iron.

I hope that these three different dolls and three different starting points will equip and inspire you to develop your own creative style.

Opposite: This dramatic stump doll is dressed in fabric created using crossway waves (see page 51).

Basic tools and equipment

For all the dolls in this book you will need the following basic set of tools and equipment:

- **Freezer paper** for making pattern templates.
- **Sharp H pencil or mechanical pencil** for drawing sharp, accurate lines.
- **Small paper scissors** for cutting intricate paper shapes.
- **Sharp fabric scissors.** Keep two pairs: large for speed and small for accuracy.
- **Fabric** for making heads and hands: 100% cotton fabric has an amount of stretch and will mold nicely into shape, unlike polyester-cotton blends, which do not give a smooth finish.
- **Forceps** are useful for gripping fabric and turning things inside out. These come in various shapes and sizes and can be obtained from doll suppliers, tool shops, or fly-fishing suppliers.
- **Finger-turning tools** are an essential for turning intricate fingers inside out. They consist of a tube and a rod. Two useful sizes are: ⅛in (4mm) tube and ¹⁄₁₆in (2mm) rod; ³⁄₃₂in (3mm) tube and ³⁄₆₄in (1.5mm) rod.
- **Stuffing fork or chopstick** for pushing stuffing into limbs and heads.
- **Good-quality polyester stuffing.** A soft, springy stuffing will give a smooth finish.
- **Soft coloring pencils** for coloring faces (see "Drawing flat faces" on page 36).
- **Waterproof and fade-proof pens** for drawing faces on fabric: size 0.5 and 0.3, in black, for outlining and 0.3 in red for lips.
- **Acrylic spray coating** will seal colored pencils and stop them from smudging.
- **Fabric eraser** for erasing pencil marks on fabric.
- **Good-quality polyester thread** for general sewing.
- **Quilting or strong thread** for needle-sculpting.
- **Long fine darning needles** in sizes 1 to 5.
- **Chenille stems or pipe cleaners** for inserting into fingers to make them flexible.
- **Felting needles** for attaching wool fibers for hair.
- **Liquid seam sealants, such as Fray Check** are fabric sealants that will stop fabric from fraying and enable you to clip very close to the stitch line. This ensures that intricate shapes can be turned through without fraying. Use this product very sparingly as it hardens the fabric, which then becomes more difficult to turn through. Cut the end off a toothpick and use the blunt end to apply the sealant. Do not squirt straight from the bottle.
- **Embroidery hoop or frame** for stretching fabric for machine embroidery.
- **Wonder Under (Bondaweb)** a double-sided adhesive web with a protective paper backing. It is used to secure fabric onto a background before stitching.
- **Parchment paper, or non-stick baking paper** is used to protect your fabric from a hot iron. This can be obtained from supermarkets.

Opposite: The hair on this wired doll was created using a felting needle (see page 125).

General information

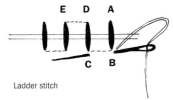

Pattern symbols

Ladder stitch

The following instructions are basic doll-making principles and apply to all the dolls in this book.

Note in **Diagram 1** that:

- A = cutting line
- B = stitching line
- C = straight grain line—the straight grain line runs parallel to the selvedge edge or finished edge of the fabric, not the cut edge
- D = clip seams—this will ease the fabric and allow it to stretch around intricate shapes, such as neck, waist, elbow, nose and fingers
- E = balance marks, which match to corresponding balance marks on another pattern piece

Stitching

Stitch length and type

For normal stitch length use ⅟₁₆in (2.0mm). When stitching the body, limbs and head, use a very small stitch, about ⅜₁₆in (1.50mm). This will provide a strong seam that will not burst open when you are stuffing the doll. Hand stitching, no matter how small, is just not strong enough.

Ladder stitch: This is an excellent stitch for closing a seam or opening, as it is virtually invisible.

Seam allowance

For normal seams leave ⅛in (0.3cm). For intricate pieces such as hands and heads, leave slightly under ⅛in (0.3cm). Too big a seam allowance will give you a lumpy finish when stuffed. Too small and it will split when stuffed.

Threads

Use a good quality polyester thread. Always use a thread that matches your fabric. If you don't, you will find that the stitching will show through when you stuff your doll. It is a shame to spoil all your hard work by letting the stitching show.

Ladder-stitch method

1 Start at A.
2 Stitch over the fabric to B.
3 Stitch under the fabric to C.
4 Stitch over the fabric to D.
5 Stitch to E, etc.

TIP When you have done three or four stitches, pull the thread gently and this will close the opening with an almost invisible finish.

Using the patterns

It is well worth taking a little time to look at the pattern and familiarizing yourself with the pieces.
• Note that some pattern pieces have a seam allowance and some do not.
• Note any information on the pattern, such as openings, grain line, number of pieces.
• Always match the straight grain line on the pattern to the straight grain of the fabric. If you don't do this, your doll's head and limbs may turn out to be a different shape from the original patterns.

The Freezer-paper Method

I like to use the freezer-paper method to transfer my patterns onto fabric as it provides a stable and accurate foundation for stitching. Here's how it is done:

Cutting out the pieces

1 Lay the freezer paper shiny side down onto the pattern.
2 With a mechanical pencil or hard sharp (H) pencil, trace around the pattern piece. Note any relevant information, such as grain lines, openings, and balance marks.
3 Cut out the freezer paper accurately.
4 Place shiny side down onto a double layer of fabric and iron with a medium-hot iron. This will now remain securely in place and provide you with an accurate shape to stitch around.
5 Using a very small stitch, ⅟₁₆in (1.5mm), stitch right along the edge of the freezer paper.
6 Peel the freezer paper away (this can be used several times).
7 Cut out the fabric with the appropriate seam allowance.

If you do not wish to use the freezer-paper method, you can trace the pattern onto paper, pin onto a double layer of fabric and trace around the shape.

Joining the pattern pieces

In order to complete some of the pattern pieces they will need to be joined together first. Trace and cut out both pieces and match up the balance marks; use sticky tape to stick the pieces together to complete the pattern, as shown in the diagram.

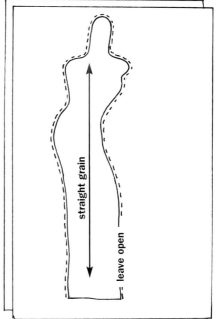

Using the pattern on a double layer of fabric

Joining the pattern pieces

Stuffing the doll

There are many makes of stuffing on the market but you need to find a light, bouncy polyester stuffing. I use Super Poly Stuffing. Some stuffing is dense when compressed, and gives a lumpy, cellulite-like finish—and we don't want cellulite! Find yourself a stuffing tool that suits you—a chopstick or a commercial toy-stuffing tool, something you are comfortable using.

1 Take a chopstick or other stuffing tool and gently press it against the inside seam. This will give you a nice smooth line and a better finish to your limbs.
2 Take as much stuffing as will go through the opening and maneuver it to the required area. Push it into the outside edges first and then fill in the inside area. This method will produce a smooth, firm finish. For intricate areas, insert a small amount of stuffing at a time.

TIP The body and limbs should be stuffed very firmly. This will prevent them sagging later.

Machine embroidery

Free-machine Stitching

Free-machine stitching means that you can stitch in any direction to create wonderful decorative effects. You are in control and not the sewing machine. The basics are simple, but the various techniques and possibilities are endless. With practice you can achieve amazing results.

For normal stitching, the fabric is held between the presser foot and the teeth (feed dog). This makes the material move forward under the material. To enable you to do free-machine stitching, you have to:

1 Lower the feed dog.
2 Remove the presser foot.
3 Thread the machine as normal.
4 Set the stitch length to 0. From now on the movement of the embroidery hoop will determine the stitch length.
5 Stretch the fabric drum-tight in an embroidery hoop.
6 Put the embroidery-hoop-framed fabric under the needle.
7 Bring the bobbin thread up by turning the hand wheel toward you. If you omit this process, you may get a tangle underneath.
8 Lower the presser foot and start machine stitching, running the machine fast and moving the frame around as required.

Right: Transfer-painted fabric and free-machine embroidery were used to create the fabric for this doll. Motifs cut out using a soldering iron were twisted around the arms.

Free-machine embroidery checklist

Top Tension: Normal

Bobbin: Normal

Presser foot: Off

Feed dog: Lowered

Stitch length: 0

Stitch width: 0

Fabric: Framed

Needle size: 90–100

chapter one
Stump Dolls

Right: The base fabric for this doll was made by layering different fabrics, free-machine stitching, and burning back with a heat gun. Stitched crossway structures (see page 51) add a further dimension.

The stump doll provides a starting point for any textile figure. The simple shapes provide an excellent base for decoration and embellishment. I have provided a standard pattern on the following four pages, but for a truly unique doll, you can start with any figurative reference point: perhaps an image from a fashion magazine, a photograph or a sketch.

These initial images can be traced or drawn freehand. Do not be afraid to experiment with the images until you have a shape you really like. When you are happy with the shape, trace it onto a piece of plain paper and add ¼in (0.6cm) seam allowance. This is your pattern. If your initial tracing or drawing is not big enough, enlarge it on a photocopier to the required size.

This pattern either can be sewn all the way around, to produce a flat shape, leaving a small opening for stuffing, or you can add a circular or oval base that will transform it into a three-dimensional figure that will stand up.

Materials and Equipment for the Basic Stump Doll

You will need:
- ½ yard (0.5m) calico or similar backing fabric
- ½ yard (0.5m) Wonder Under (Bondaweb)
- Small pieces of fabric, such as polyester lining, silk, satin, cotton, brocade, etc.
- Sheer nylon fabric
- Baking parchment
- Embroidery hoop
- Machine-embroidery threads that are heat resistant
- Heat tool: Only use a heat tool from a craft supplier (a hair dryer is not hot enough and, despite what any man may tell you, a hot-air gun of the type usually used for stripping paint is far too hot and can be dangerous!)
- Sand or plastic toy pellets to weight the sand bag
- 100% cotton fabric in a flesh tone for making head and hands
- Colored pencils
- Waterproof and fade-proof pens
- Acrylic spray coating
- Toy stuffing
- Forceps
- Stuffing fork

Left: Drawings simplified from fashion figures traced from magazines. The simplified versions can be used as patterns to create a uniquely shaped doll.

Stump doll patterns

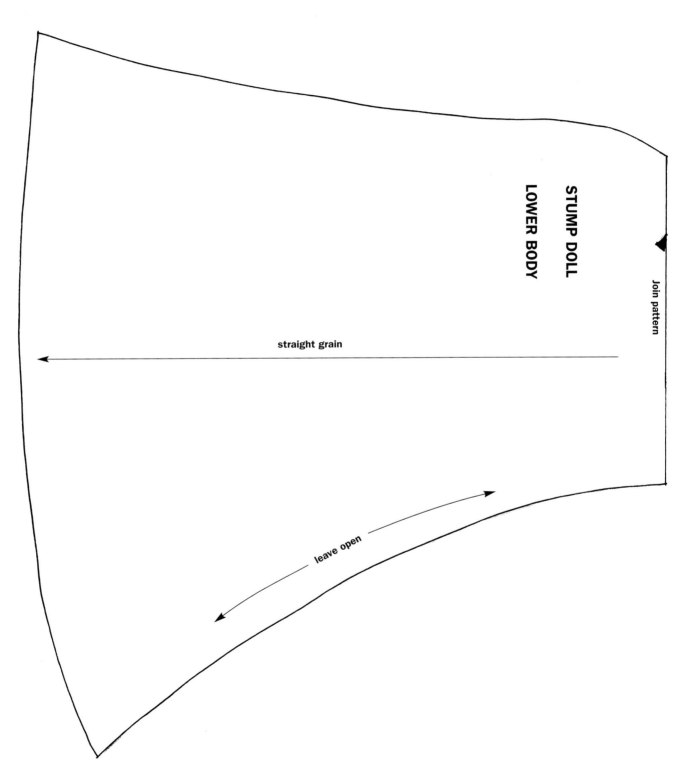

STUMP DOLL
LOWER BODY

Join pattern

straight grain

leave open

Enlarge pattern on a photocopier by 115%

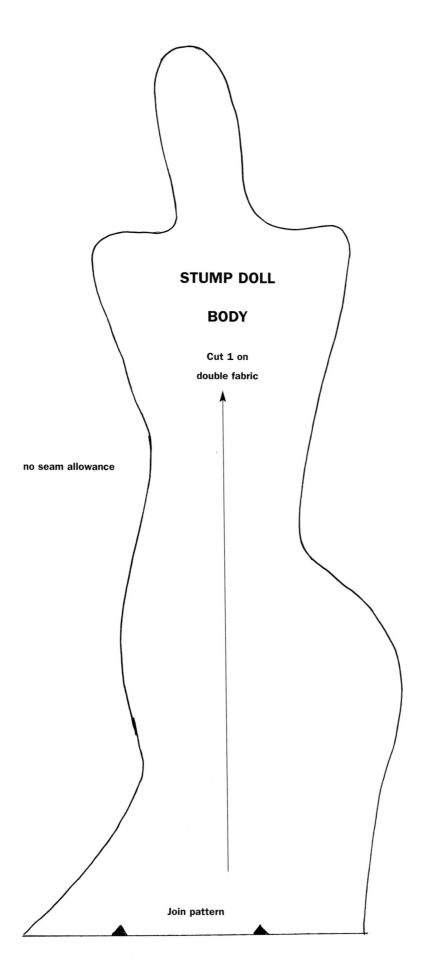

STUMP DOLL

BODY

Cut 1 on

double fabric

no seam allowance

Join pattern

Enlarge pattern on a photocopier by 115%

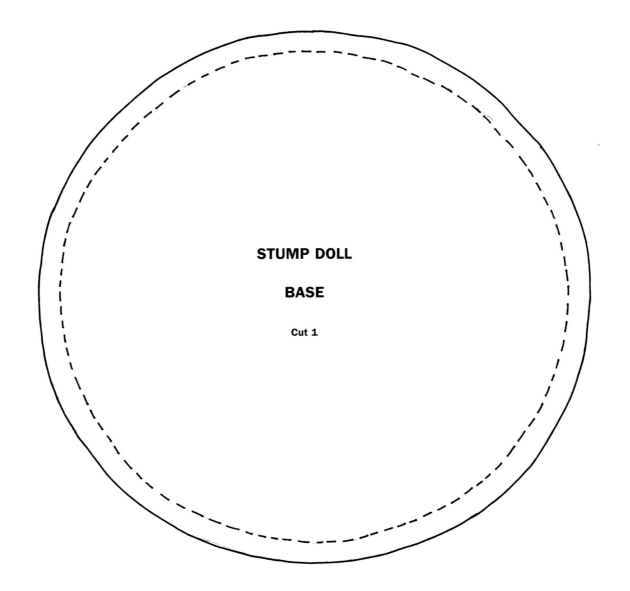

STUMP DOLL

BASE

Cut 1

Enlarge patterns on a photocopier by 115%

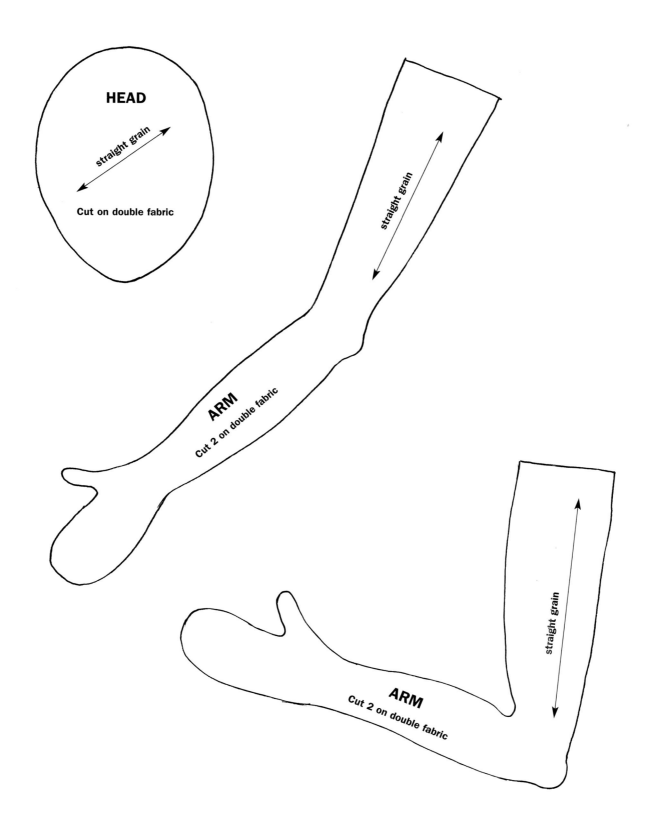

HEAD

straight grain

Cut on double fabric

ARM

Cut 2 on double fabric

straight grain

ARM

Cut 2 on double fabric

straight grain

Enlarge patterns on a photocopier by 115%

Making layered background fabrics

The next step is to create some fabric for the body of your doll. A simple doll can be greatly enhanced by using exciting fabrics and, although there are many fantastic fabrics on the market today, there is nothing quite as satisfying as creating your own. Experiment with a wide range of fabrics and colors to see what you can achieve: Shiny satins and linings provide a contrast to tweeds and velvets; lace and brocades add extra texture. This experimentation gives you the freedom to choose your own color schemes, create texture and develop your own ideas. The fabrics in this section have been used to make the body of the doll, then extra embellishment has been added.

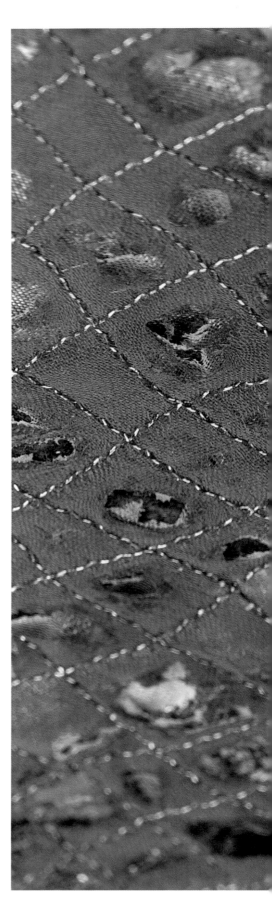

Right: Small pieces of gold and blue fabric were overlaid with sheer nylon and straight-stitched with metallic thread. The whole piece was then zapped with a heat gun to reveal the fabrics underneath.

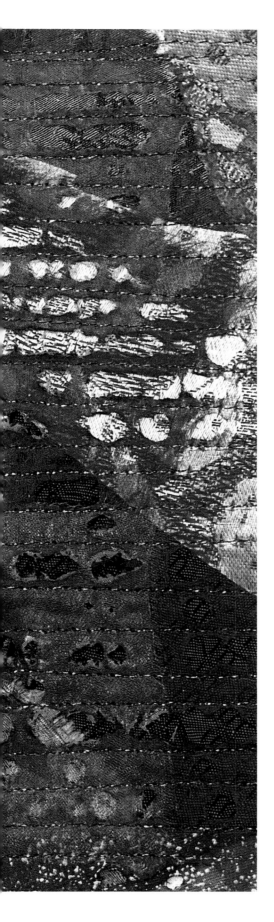

This layering technique is one of my favorites because it is so incredibly versatile. It enables you to explore a huge variety of colors and textures. The technique is about layering fabrics, and because the background will be covered with a layer of sheer nylon, which in turn will be burned back, it is important to consider carefully the colors you choose for it. Mixing many colors together on one background will produce bold, vibrant effects, while using different tones of one color will give you a more muted or subtle effect.

Once you have made your basic background fabric, you will need to consider the next layer. This is a sheer piece of nylon fabric, some of which will eventually be burned away with a heat gun. This fabric is an integral part of the design and it is important to consider the color you choose, because different colors will change the nature of the original background. The samples on this page and pages 22–23 started with the same background, but by using a different colored nylon and a different stitch, two completely different fabrics have been produced.

It is a good idea to experiment with different colors by laying them on top of the background; you can determine the finished effect before you start sewing. The stitching will also determine the end result of your work. A close free-machine stitch pattern will give a denser effect to the top layer. A more open stitch pattern will expose more of the background. Straight stitching can also be very effective; lines and grids will produce lovely effects.

Left: The background of this piece was made up in the contrasting colors blue and yellow. A blue sheer nylon fabric was used on top and rows of straight stitching were added, then the whole piece was zapped with a heat gun.

It is not always easy to predict what the exact result will be but I always am pleased with the end product. I would suggest that you experiment with some sample pieces first: You may find that one of your samples will inspire the entire theme of your doll.

These lush layered fabrics are ideal for making stump dolls. They will transform any simple shape into a fabulous figure that can be further embellished and decorated. Hand stitching couched wires and handmade cords can add a final dimension to your work.

Technique

1 Cut a piece of calico large enough to accommodate the back and front of the body pattern.
2 Cut a piece of Wonder Under (Bondaweb) the same size as the calico and place it web side down onto the calico.
3 On a medium to hot setting, iron the Wonder Under (Bondaweb) onto the calico. You will be ironing onto the paper side of the Wonder Under (Bondaweb).
4 Peel the paper away (exposing the adhesive web) and lay squares, strips or random pieces of fabric on top.
5 Cover with a piece of sheer nylon fabric and free machine on top of this sandwich of fabric.
6 Alternatively, you can use straight stitch with the feed dog up to create patterns.
7 Take a craft heat gun and zap until you have the desired effect. This will give you a fabric that can be worked into with further stitching and embellishment.

TIP Because we will be using a craft heat gun to distress this work, you must use threads that are heat resistant. Use cotton or metallic threads and, if you are unsure about them, test before you start machine stitching.

Opposite: Long, irregularly shaped strips of fabric were used to make the background of this piece. Pink sheer nylon was added on top, and random free-machine stitching in a metallic thread was added before the piece was zapped. Layers of fly stitching were added for extra texture.

A
 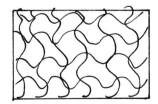 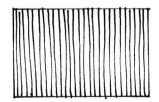

B
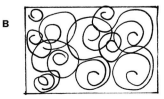 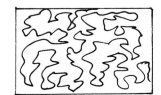 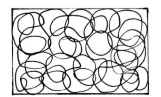

Left: Some ideas for stitch patterns.

Above: This piece of fabric was created by laying down random shapes of fabric (left), covering them with black nylon fabric and free-machine stitching on top (middle). The whole piece was then zapped with a heat gun (right).

Here are some samples that I made using this technique:

Using tones of gold and brown a background was made up of random shapes of satin, polyester lining, brocade and Lurex wool. This was then covered with a black sheer nylon. Random free stitching in a metallic thread was added before the piece was zapped with a heat gun, exposing rich textures underneath. The three stages of the process are shown on the left.

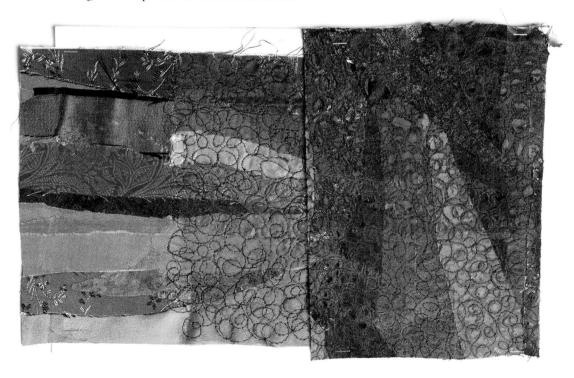

Long irregular strips of fabric were used for the background of this piece. Pink sheer nylon was added on top and random free-machine stitching in a metallic thread was added, before the piece was zapped. The three stages of the process are shown in the picture above.

Above: Strips of fabric were used to create the background (left), before a second layer of pink nylon and free-machine stitching were added (middle). A heat gun was used to distress the fabric and reveal the colors beneath (right).

Use of Color

I love to experiment with color when making background fabrics. I find the colors used can determine the "character" of the finished doll—bright, jewel-like colors make the doll look happy, darker ones inject a note of drama, or pale ones can make a doll look more ethereal and fairy-like. Consider also whether you would like to use warmer tones, cooler tones, or contrasting colors for maximum visual impact.

The fabric below (also shown in its entirety on page 26) has been worked in warm pinks and purples. A swirly pattern was free-machine stitched over the top and the piece was then embellished with a random scattering of fly stitch in thread that has been random-dyed by hand.

The background of the piece on the opposite page (also shown on pages 22–23) was made up in the contrasting colors blue and yellow. A blue nylon sheer was used on top and rows of straight stitching were added in a grid pattern, proving that simple stitching can be very effective in adding texture.

Opposite: Detail of fabric shown on pages 22-23.

Opposite: Detail of fabric shown on page 26.

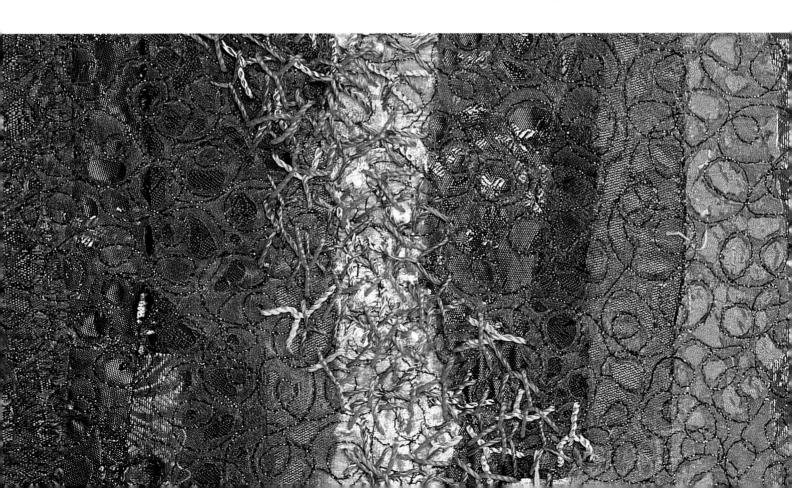

Constructing the stump doll

1 Use the freezer-paper method described on page 11 to transfer the pattern to the fabric, and refer to the general pattern and construction techniques on page 10. Cut out the pattern with an ¼in (0.6cm) seam allowance.

2 Clip the neck and waist curves as shown in the diagram below.

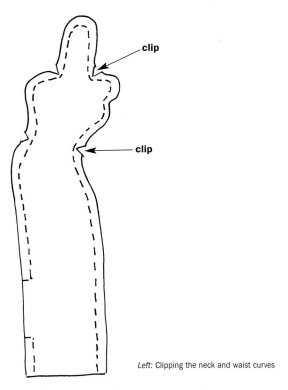

Left: Clipping the neck and waist curves

3 Pin in the base as shown in the diagram, and machine around.

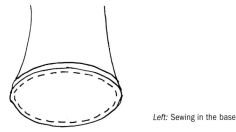

Left: Sewing in the base

4 Turn the body through to the right side.

5 Insert the sandbag (see instructions on the opposite page for making a sandbag) through the side opening.

6 Stuff the doll very firmly.

7 Close the opening with ladder stitch.

Making a Sandbag

A sandbag will give your figure some stability and help it stand upright.
Use calico or similar sturdy fabric for the bag. A pattern is given below.

1 Make a cylinder of fabric as shown in the diagram, right.

2 Machine stitch down the short side of the sandbag body.

3 Ease the circular base in, and machine stitch in place.

4 Turn inside out and half-fill with sand or plastic toy pellets.

5 Fold in both sides of the top and machine stitch across as shown in the
diagram.

TIP You can fill your bag with sand, plastic toy pellets, split
peas or birdseed, but beware, if the latter gets damp, it
will sprout!

Stitching the sandbag together

Stitching the stuffed sandbag

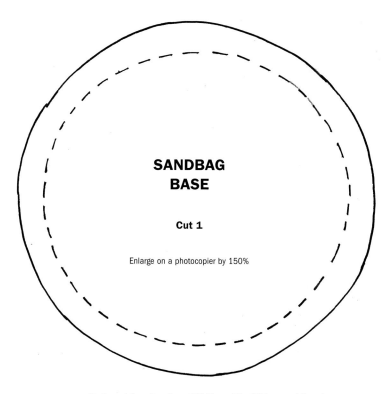

**SANDBAG
BASE**

Cut 1

Enlarge on a photocopier by 150%

Cut a strip of calico 10½in x 5in (27cm x 13cm)

for the body of the bag

Making mitten hands

Hands can be hard to make but, with a little care and patience, should not be too problematical. Although mitten hands are simple to make, they can look very effective.

1 Use the freezer-paper method as described on page 11.
2 Apply a small dot of liquid seam sealant at the thumb (see diagram), and leave to dry.
3 Cut out with ⅛in (0.3cm) seam allowance.
4 Clip into the thumb and elbow as shown in the diagram.
5 Stuff firmly.
6 Mark the position of the fingers, as shown in the diagram, either with pins or with a water-soluble pen.
7 Using a single, strong, flesh-colored thread, stitch backward and forward right through the hand, creating a continuous line of stitching.
8 Don't stitch right to the end of the fingers but take a stitch over the end of the finger, and pull gently. Repeat this stitch. This will create the impression of separate fingers.

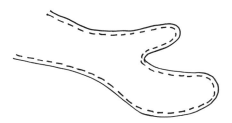

Applying liquid seam sealant at the thumb

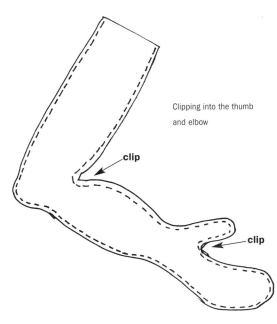

Clipping into the thumb and elbow

clip

clip

Marking the position of the fingers

Stitching over the end of the fingers and pulling gently

Opposite: Mitten hands can look very effective on your doll.

Making a flat face

1 Using the freezer-paper method and a small stitch, machine stitch all the way around the head as shown in the diagram.

2 Cut out with ⅛in (0.3cm) seam allowance.

3 Cut a 1in (2.5cm) slit in the back of the head and turn the head inside out through this slit.

4 Stuff firmly and close the opening.

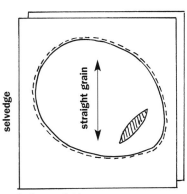

Cutting out a flat face

Drawing Flat Faces

Drawing faces is the part of doll making that people find most troublesome, but if you take your time and relax, it will become an enjoyable experience. It is important to practice drawing faces on a piece of fabric first; don't be tempted to start on the finished head. I always make several heads for any one doll and choose the one I like best. By practicing the techniques and experimenting, you will start to develop your own style. See the list below for a useful range of colors.

Equipment
- Soft coloring pencils, which will shade and blend easily (Derwent Inktense and Derwent Coloursoft work well on cotton cloth)

Useful colors for faces
- Ocher
- Terra-cotta
- Peach
- Sepia
- Light and dark blue
- Light and dark green
- Scarlet
- Magenta
- White
- Violet

Waterproof and fade-proof pens come in different thicknesses:
- Black 005 and 05
- Brown 005
- Red 005

- Fabric eraser

TIP You can also use gel pens, but always test them on fabric first to make sure they do not bleed.

Mapping out the face

It is a good idea to map out the features of the face before you start to color them in.

By following a few basic rules and using simple shapes, it is possible to produce a well-constructed face.

1 Use an ocher colored pencil to lightly draw in the basic outline. This will be lost when the flesh tones are added and blended in.
2 Draw a vertical line down the center of the head, as shown in the diagram.
3 Draw a horizontal line for the eye line, which is about halfway down the head.
4 Draw in the nose line and mouth line.

The basic layout of the face

Right: Expressive hand-drawn and colored faces can bring your doll to life. This one has an air of wistfulness.

Eyes

1 Mark the pupils of the eye by placing a dot halfway along each eye line.
2 Using the eye dot as the center, draw a circle to represent the pupil (see diagram, right).
3 Draw an outer circle to represent the iris.
4 Draw a curved upper lid line, skimming over the top of the iris (see diagram, right).
5 Draw a lower lid line, just touching the bottom of the iris. Do not complete this line but leave a gap toward the inner eye.
6 Draw in the eye socket and eyebrow, as shown in the diagram, below right.

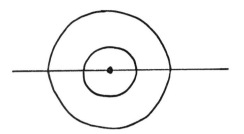

Using the eye dot as the center

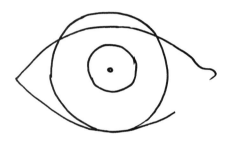

Drawing a curved upper lid line

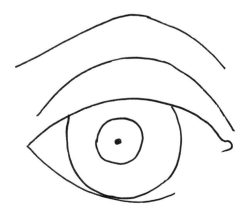

Drawing the eye socket and eyebrow

Nose

1 Draw a large circle and two smaller circles to form the nose (see diagram).

2 Draw in the bridge of the nose. Make it narrower at the top and wider at the bottom.

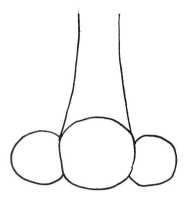

Drawing the outline of the nose

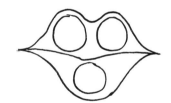

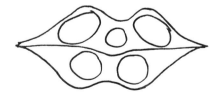

Mouth

The mouth can be constructed by using a combination of ovals and circles. Different combinations will give you different mouths.

1 Start by drawing ovals and circles, as in the diagrams, left.

2 Using the ovals and circles as a guide, outline the mouth.

3 Draw in the center of the mouth.

4 Now that the nose and mouth are in place, you can draw in the philtrum under the nose.

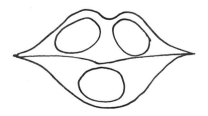

Constructing the mouth using circles and ovals

The basic facial features

Coloring in the Features

Now you have the basic features mapped out in ocher pencil (see diagram, left, for the whole face), you are ready to color them in. To achieve depth and contours with coloring, always use several shades of a color on any one area. For example, if you are coloring blue eyes, use several shades of blue and even a touch of brown to give real depth to the darkest area.

Experiment with colors on your practice piece. You will be surprised how blending colors can change your finished effect.

Eyes

1 Color in the iris using a pale color first, and leaving an uncolored section at the bottom.
2 Use a darker color on the top half of the iris.
3 Using a black pen, fill in the pupil.
4 Outline the iris with a fine black pen.
5 Outline the eyelid with a black pen, making the line thicker at outer edge.
6 Use a fine brown pen to draw the socket line and radiating lines around the pupil.
7 Paint in the highlights with white fabric paint. Also, paint in the whites of the eyes.
8 Using a sepia pencil, shade along the eye-socket line and the inside and outside corners of the eye.
9 Color can be added to the eyelid at this point.
10 With a fine black pen, draw in the eyelashes by flicking the lines upward. Make several rows of eyelashes.
11 Build up the eyebrows by completing several rows of short lines.

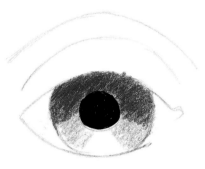

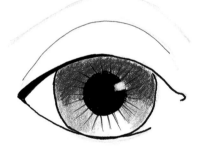

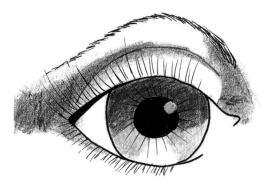

Right: Coloring the eye.

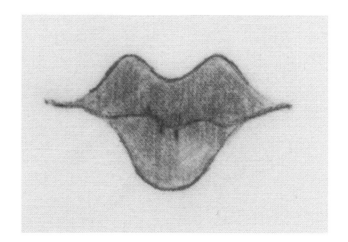

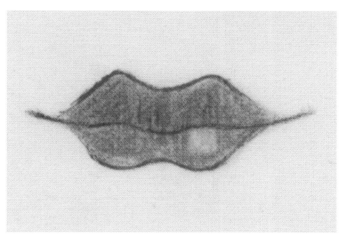

Above and left: Coloring the lips

Lips

Use several shades of red to color the lips.

1 Color in the lips, blending the two colors together, then darken the top lip.

2 With a red pen, draw in lines to give the mouth some definition (see diagram).

3 Finish the lips by adding soft highlights with a white pencil.

Right and opposite: Two faces at different stages of completion.

Face

1 Using an ocher pencil, shade down the side of the nose and the outside edge of each nose circle.

2 Shade the top of the forehead, down the side of the face, under the lower lip.

3 Use a terra-cotta pencil to darken the same area, but don't quite cover the ocher.

4 Use two shades of red to color the cheek area.

5 Finally, use white to highlight the center of the nose, each nostril, and the end of the nose. (This may look a little harsh, but when it is blended together, it will produce subtle flesh tones.)

6 Take a small piece of cotton cloth and rub the surface gently until the colors blend together.

7 Take a brown pen and draw in the nose holes and the sides of the nostrils.

8 With a sepia pencil, lightly shade in the nose holes.

9 Finally, seal with acrylic fabric spray.

Drawing in the nostrils

Attaching the Head

Push the neck into the opening of the head and arrange into a suitable position before stitching into place with ladder stitch. See Stitching, page 10, and the diagram, right.

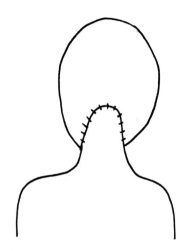

Attaching the head

Attaching the Arms

The arms on this doll have a straight top. This means that they can be posed at a variety of angles before you sew them in.

1 Turn the top of the arm under and position it onto the shoulder.

2 Add more stuffing to plump up the arm if required.

3 Ladder-stitch into place (see diagram below).

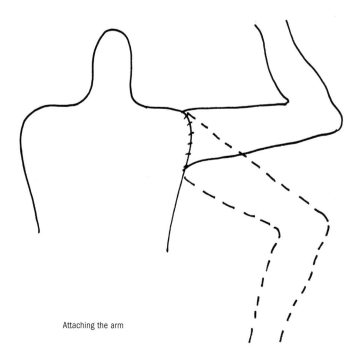

Attaching the arm

Machine-wrapped cords and braids

Cords and braids can give a wonderful textured appearance to your doll. The effectiveness of any braid or cord is dependent on the yarns or threads that are used.

A cord is made by covering a core with dense zigzag stitching; by experimenting with different machine threads you can produce some beautiful effects. Experiment with shiny, variegated and metallic threads. Mix and match the threads; there are many possibilities. Once the cord is made, it can be used for couching down onto a background fabric or as wrapping decoration on a doll. Double strands of cords and knotted cords add another dimension to any doll—a rich and exciting texture.

Looser braids can be made by using yarns, threads, or strips of fabric as the core and stitching randomly along this core. The effectiveness of the braid will depend on the yarns you have chosen. Again these braids can be used for wrapping or they also can make wonderful hats and hair.

Right: A variety of yarns and threads were used to make these machine-wrapped braids. Gaps have been left between the stitching so that the yarns are exposed in places.

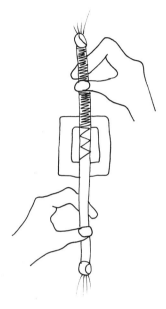

Preventing the bobbin thread disappearing into
the bobbin holder

Here is a simple technique from which you can produce a great variety of sumptuous braids and cords. Experiment with string, wool, and strips of fabric, raffia, and fancy yarns. Use singly or bundle several together.

1 Remove the presser foot and replace with a darning or embroidery foot.

2 Lower the feed dog.

3 Select a type of thread or cord for the core of your braid.

4 Tie a knot in each end.

5 Set your machine to the appropriate zigzag width. (The zigzag must be wide enough to pass on either side of the core.)

6 To prevent the bobbin thread disappearing into the bobbin holder, hold the top and bottom threads together with the core. Hold the core taut with one hand at the back of the machine.

7 Lower the presser foot and start to machine stitch, moving carefully backward and forward. The stitching can be quite close or very dense, depending on what you want to achieve.

TIP • **Experiment with matte, shiny, and metallic threads.**
 • **Try leaving spaces and gaps so the core shows through.**

Opposite: Machine-made cords are used to dramatic effect on this doll.

Pages 48–49: Fine copper wire was couched onto a textured background and then knotted machine-made cords were added to create deep textures.

Above: These machine-wrapped braids were made by mixing metallic threads, yarns and strips of torn fabric together.

Right: Copper wire and machine-wrapped metallic braids were couched down to create this opulent fabric.

Crossway waves and structures

Crossway waves create a very organic-looking appearance and the results will depend on the type of fabrics you use. A firmer fabric such as polyester satin will produce an entirely different effect from fine silk or stiff organdy. When these fabrics are combined, they will react with and against each other to produce some surprising results. Consider the texture of your fabrics as well as the colors. Combine rough and smooth fabrics as well as shiny and matte ones.

The stitching also plays an important part in this technique. Stitching in a uniform and even manner will produce some interesting results, but if you stitch randomly on the cross grain of the fabric, the results will be a lot more spectacular.

Above: A variety of fabrics were stitched on the cross grain to create these fluid wavy stuctures, which were then draped around this stump doll.

Below: Crossway waves can lend a real sense of structure to your work.

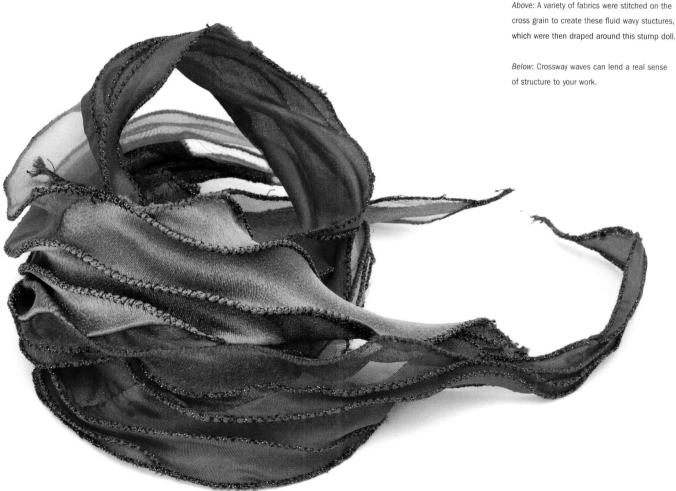

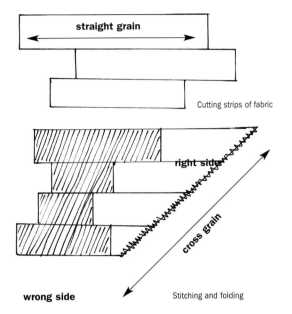

straight grain

Cutting strips of fabric

right side

cross grain

wrong side   Stitching and folding

The technique is based on the traditional dressmakers' bias or crossway strip. By combining different fabrics and exploring stitching on the cross grain, you can produce some wonderful organic shapes and structures. Experiment with fabrics of different weights and types, such as lining fabric, silk, sheer nylon, organza, and scrim.

1 Cut strips of fabric and machine together in a random way.
2 Fold across at right angles to find the bias or cross grain.
3 Either straight-stitch close to the edge of the fold or zigzag on the edge of the fold.
4 Continue to fold and stitch the whole piece of fabric in this way. You do not need to have your folds even or the same distance apart—the more random the folding and stitching, the more interesting the result.

This can become a compulsive technique; an amazing variety of structures can be achieved by varying fabric combinations.

The polyester satin produced a strong structural shape in the piece shown at the bottom of page 51, pulling against the sheer nylon fabric and polyester lining. The shape was determined by the combination of these fabrics. This structure has many possibilities for wrapping around a figure or as a costume.

The fabrics used in the piece shown opposite were all of a similar weight, and the result is a much softer structure.

Opposite: Polyester lining fabric, sheer nylon and scrim were joined together, and then zigzag stitched on the cross grain to create these intriguing organic structures.

chapter two

Wired Dolls

Right: Plaited braids and cords were added to this wired doll and woolen yarns were couched down with buttonhole stitch.

A wired doll has a simple wire armature that means that it can be posed in a variety of positions. I like to use images of dancers and acrobats as sources of inspiration to create movement and flow.

The wrapping technique used to cover the armature makes this doll a perfect vehicle for decorative hand stitching and embellishment. Plaited braids, twisted cords, rouleau tubes, frills and puffs also add another dimension.

Don't be afraid to experiment with a variety of fabrics, anything from fine nylons to rich velvets. You will be surprised at the different effects you can achieve by using this technique.

Materials and Equipment for the Basic Wired Doll

You will need:

- Wire: The gauge of the wire is crucial to this technique. If it is too thin, your figure will not support itself. Generally I use 1.6mm for a tall doll of 23 inches (58cm) and 1.25mm for a smaller doll. Wire is available from metal suppliers, hardware stores, and garden centers.

TIP Don't be tempted to buy green garden wire; it is not firm enough.

- Wire cutters or pliers
- ½ yard (0.5m) of two-ounce polyester batting
- ½ yard (0.5m) fabric. To achieve a good smooth finish when wrapping, it is best to use stretchy fabric. Most stretch fabric will work, but some will "roll" when you pull it and some will easily develop runs, so always test before you buy. Don't be afraid to buy patterned fabric, as it will be cut into strips and wrapped, creating a totally different effect. The most hideous fabrics can look fabulous.
- ¼ yard (0.25m) flesh-colored 100% cotton fabric for the head and hands
- Polyester stuffing
- Flesh-colored quilting thread or similar for needle-sculpting
- Long fine darning needle
- Colored pencils
- Waterproof and fade-proof pens
- Finger-turning tools
- Stuffing fork
- Forceps
- Chenille stems or pipe cleaners
- Fancy yarns and threads for embellishment

Making the armature

1 Draw the basic armature pattern (see diagram) onto a large piece of paper to use as a guide. The measurements are approximate. I like to use a figure with longer legs, so experiment with body proportions and create your own perfect shape.

2 For a 23in (58cm) doll, cut a piece of 1.6mm wire about 11 feet (3.5m) long.

3 Bend the wire in half, lay it down on the pattern, follow the shape of the head and twist it together to form the head.

4 Using the pattern as a guide, take one length of wire and make the arm, twist around the neck, and continue with the same length of wire to form the body and legs. Wind any excess wire around the body.

5 Repeat this process with the other piece of wire.

6 Using flat-nosed pliers, squash the ends of the arms and legs to secure them.

Once you have made your wire armature, it is time to start wrapping.

Bending the wire to form the head

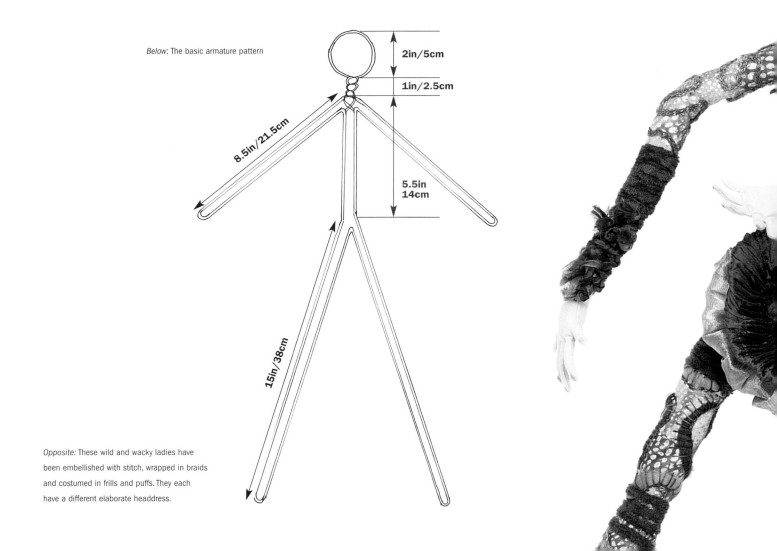

Below: The basic armature pattern

2in/5cm

1in/2.5cm

8.5in/21.5cm

5.5in
14cm

15in/38cm

Opposite: These wild and wacky ladies have been embellished with stitch, wrapped in braids and costumed in frills and puffs. They each have a different elaborate headdress.

Left: Rich textures were created on this wired doll by using a combination of velvets and satins and rouleau and frill techniques.

Wrapping techniques

1 Cut polyester batting into strips approximately 1¼ inches (3cm) wide.

2 Working at an angle, wrap up and down the armature with the polyester batting, starting with the head ring.

TIP Keep the wadding taut to create a firm finish. If your wrapping is loose, your finish will be spongy and may become dimpled when you stitch into it.

3 Continue to wrap until you have created a shape you like.
   You can make your figure thin or you can build up muscles and curves.
   It is at this point that your figure really takes on a character of its own.

TIP Don't put too much wadding on the ends of the arms as you will be attaching the hands at this point.

4 When you are satisfied with the shape, take a long darning needle and polyester thread and stitch randomly backward and forward through the figure. This doesn't have to look neat; it is just to secure the wadding.

5 At this point, it is best to make and attach the hands (see page 62). When the hands are attached, use the same wrapping technique to cover the figure with 1–1½ inch (2.5–4cm) strips of fabric, this time securing it with a tiny stitch in a matching thread.

TIP Do not pull your stitches too tight, or you may create the appearance of cellulite!

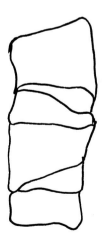

Above: It is not always necessary to make a complicated shoe. This simple wrapped toe is very effective.

Left: Wrapping up and down the armature.

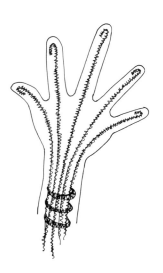

Stitching the hand

rod

Inserting the tube

Inserting chenille stems

Making hands with fingers

There are not many tools to buy for doll making, but I would recommend that you invest in a set of finger-turning tools (see Basic tools and equipment, page 8). They do require a little practice but are invaluable.

Use the freezer-paper method (see page 11) to make the hands.

Make sure that you have two stitches across the top of each finger and in between each finger, otherwise you will have a very difficult job turning the finger through.

1 Using a blunt toothpick, put a blob of liquid seam sealant in between each finger and leave to dry.
2 Clip very closely to the stitching in between each finger.
3 Insert the tube inside a finger (see diagram).

TIP If you rest the end of the tube against your stomach you will have both hands free to turn the fingers through.

4 Take the rod and hold it against the top of the finger. Start to roll the finger up the rod. Roll a little at a time. Do not try to push the whole finger from the bottom. Note that you are not trying to force the fabric down the tube, but are rolling the fabric up the tube.
5 Once all the fingers are turned through, take a pair of forceps, grip the finger and turn it inside out.
6 Measure from the fingertip to the wrist and cut five chenille stems this length.
7 Turn over at one end and push one chenille stem into each finger (see diagram).

TIP Inserting chenille stems into the fingers means that the fingers can be posed and will look more realistic. Use a chenille stem that will fit the fingers. They come in different thicknesses, about ¼in (9mm) being the most useful. If you have thinner stems, you can use them double. If you wish, you can insert a tiny amount of stuffing into each finger to give them further plumpness.

8 Wrap one stem around the other five to create a slim bundle that will be inserted into the arm.
9 Add some stuffing to the back and front of the hand, but don't overdo it as you don't want to end up with a "bunch of bananas."

Above: Hands with individual fingers will always add extra charm to your doll, as they can be posed in a variety of expressive positions.

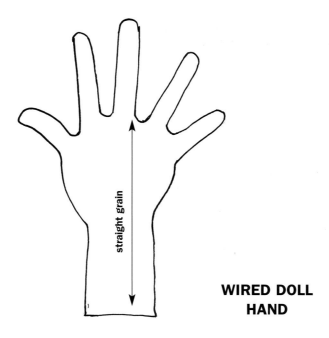

**WIRED DOLL
HAND**

Attaching the Hands

1 Push the end of the arm well down into the wrist of the hand.

2 Add a little stuffing to the hand and the wrist.

3 With a needle and a double thickness of thread, stitch backward and forward through the wrist (as shown in the diagram) and finish off by winding the thread around the wrist and securing with a couple of backstitches.

TIP Make sure you now have a right and a left hand!

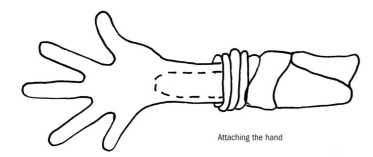

Attaching the hand

Opposite: Rich velvets, sheer nylon and polyester lining fabric were used to make the skirt for this doll. Varying the width of the frills and the texture of the fabrics will give you a more interesting result.

Making a three-dimensional head

1 Using the freezer-paper method (see page 11), iron freezer paper onto a double layer of fabric.

2 Using a very small stitch, machine stitch around the profile only.

3 Cut the profile out with an ⅛in (0.4cm) seam allowance.

4 Machine stitch down the center back of the head, leaving an opening and cut with an ⅛in (0.4cm) seam allowance.

5 Cut along the side of the head that has a seam allowance.

6 Put the front and back of the head right sides together and machine stitch all the way around the side of the face.

7 Turn through the opening at the center back.

8 Stuff firmly and close the opening.

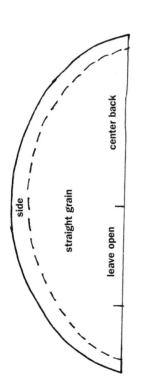

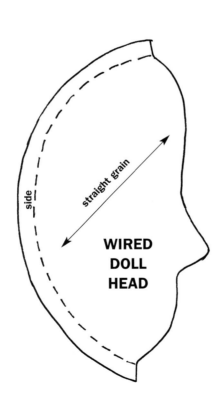

WIRED DOLL HEAD

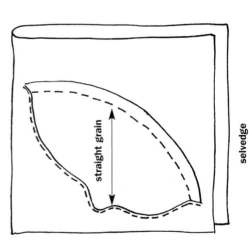

Above: Cutting the profile

Opposite: Machine-wrapped cords were wound around the body and neck of this wired doll, and layers of stitch were used to enhance the body. Finally, puffs in silk and nylon were added to create a costume.

Needle-sculpting a Three-dimensional Head

Before you start sculpting, take a good look at your doll's face to familiarize yourself with it.

• Make sure that the eyes are approximately halfway down the head.

• Use pins to mark the inner and outer eye position, nostrils and mouth.

• Using a flesh-colored soft pencil, mark the sides of the nose, keeping it narrow at the top and broader at the bottom. Make sure that you do not take it right down to the nostrils.

• The stitching should be small, but not too small or you will tear the fabric when you pull on the thread.

• Pull the stitching firmly, but not too tight or you may cause wrinkles or a very pinched-looking face.

• When you want an area of the face to hold its shape, repeat the stitch sequence twice to give it extra strength.

• Don't be afraid to go into a stitch more than once. You can return to the point more than once.

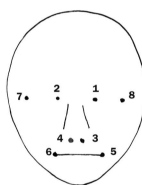

Marking out the face

Face

For the face, use a strong thread such as quilting thread or similar and a long fine darning needle.

1 Take about 1 yard (1m) of thread and knot the end.

2 Starting at the back of the head, secure with two stitches.

3 Push the needle through to the front of the head, exiting at the inner eye dot 1 (see diagram).

4 Take a small stitch in at 1 and out at 2.

5 Sew in at 2 and out at 1.

6 Repeat these steps again, pulling the thread gently.

Stitching the face

Opposite: This doll's face has been needle-sculpted. Her jaunty little headdress was created using velvet and polyester frills, which were twisted around the head. A rouleau tube was wired and made into the spiral topknot.

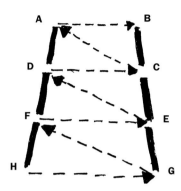

Creating the bridge of the nose

Nose

To create the bridge of the nose, sew in the following order:

• Take a small stitch in at 1 and out at A (the top of the bridge of the nose). Work backward and forward, using a backstitch. Sew in the following order:

• In at A, out at B

• In at C, out at A

• In at D, out at C

• In at E, out at D

• In at F, out at E

• In at G, out at F

• In at H, out at G.

To make the nostrils, take small stitches in the following order:

• In at G, out at 3

• In at 3, out at G

• In at G, out at 3

• In at 3, out at G

Pull the thread gently. This will form the nostril.

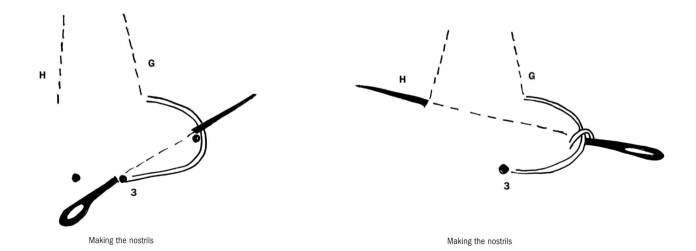

Making the nostrils

Making the nostrils

For the nose wings:

1. Mark the position with a pin.

2. Take the thread around the pin. Put the needle in at 3, out in front of the pin and the thread.

3. Take a stitch over the top of the thread, out at H.

4. Repeat this process with the other nostril, finishing at G.

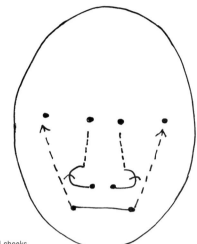

Making the mouth and cheeks

Mouth and cheeks

To make the mouth and cheeks, take a stitch and sew in the following order:

• In at G, out at 5

• In at 5, out at 8

• In at 8, out at 5

• In at 5, out at 8

• Pull thread very gently upward to form the cheek.

• Take a stitch back down to 5

To make the mouth sew in the following order:

• Take the thread over the top of the fabric to 6.

• Complete the other cheek.

• To finish off, take a stitch from 7 to the back of the head and finish off with two stitches to secure.

Coloring a three-dimensional face

The principles of coloring a three-dimensional face are basically the same as coloring a flat face (see page 40–43). However, the stitch profile and the needle-sculpting will determine the positioning of the features.

Attaching the head

When you have sculpted and colored the head, position it onto the wrapped head ring and stitch in place.

Creating texture with hand stitching

The wired and wrapped doll is ideal for hand-stitched decoration. By varying the length, width, flow and thread, you can create some exciting textural finishes on your figure.

I like to add hand stitching to fabric I have already made, to add a bit of texture and crunch. Stitch can be used to create surface decoration, highlight a particular area, give definition to outlines or simply to create pattern. It can also add color and tone, to emphasize an area or blend two or more areas together. The body shape and basic fabric of the doll will also influence your choice of stitch and thread.

Although the stitches may be simple, they can offer huge possibilities for enhancing your doll. Explore each stitch and its possibilities before you start to work on your doll. Try experimenting with threads: Any sort of thread can be used, from rayon or metallic machine threads to tubular ribbon.

Remember too that each stitch technique can be varied enormously. It is sometimes difficult to get away from the old school of thought that all stitches have to be all the same length and evenly spaced. This rule was instilled in me at school and it has taken me some time to break free from it. So explore each stitch. They could:
• vary in length and width
• be stitched formally and evenly
• be stitched randomly
• overlap and be worked in layers

Right: Layers of fly stitch were added to this background fabric for extra richness.

Opposite: Buttonhole stitch was used to add texture to this wired doll.

Pages 74–75: This fabric was transfer-painted, appliquéd and machine stitched. A simple straight stitch was added using plain and variegated threads.

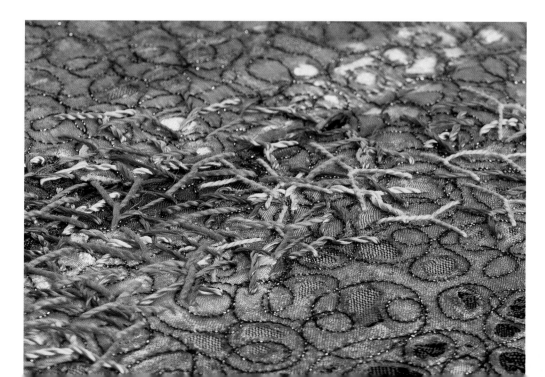

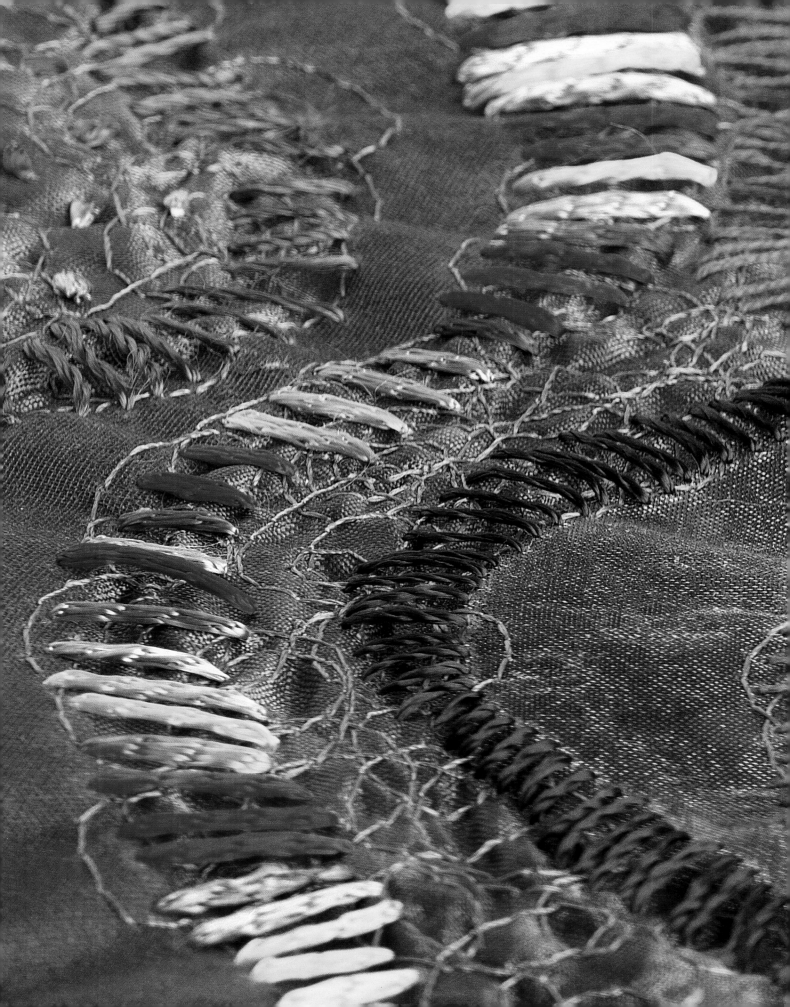

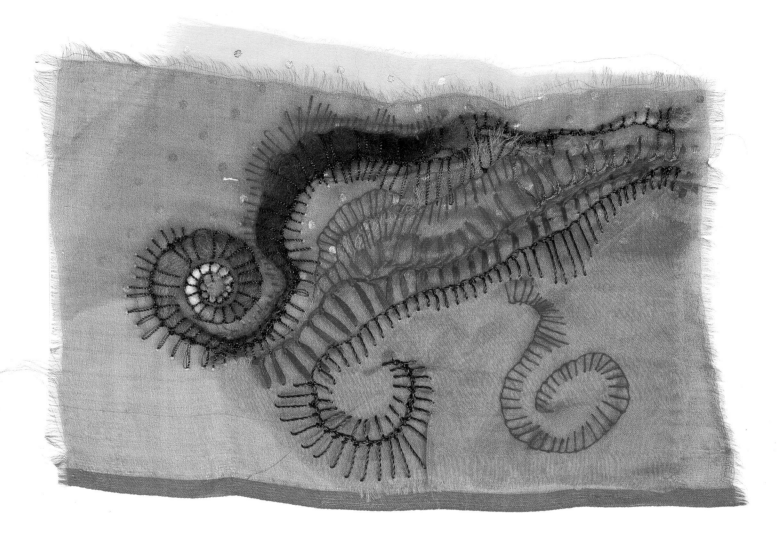

Above: Buttonhole stitch was used here to produce some very decorative effects. It is a useful stitch for couching down heavy yarns and creating flowing lines.

Here are some of the stitches you can use:

Buttonhole Stitch

I spent many hours at school trying to make buttonholes with beautifully even stitches so this sample was a bit of a challenge, but by using yarn that had both thick and thin areas I soon got used to doing both long and short stitches. The sample above shows how the stitch can be developed by:

• using it to couch down woolen yarn
• producing flowing lines
• using metallic threads, rayon threads, pearl cotton and tubular ribbon

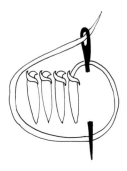

Above: Buttonhole stitch

Fly stitch

A simple but effective old favorite, fly stitch has been used in this sample (below) to develop a flowing line, using wool and metallic threads, create dense areas with formal stitching, and produce a random pattern, using metallic thread and tubular ribbon. The woolen fleece was attached with metallic thread.

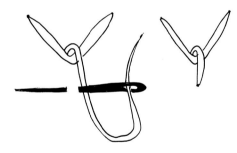

Above and below: Fly Stitch

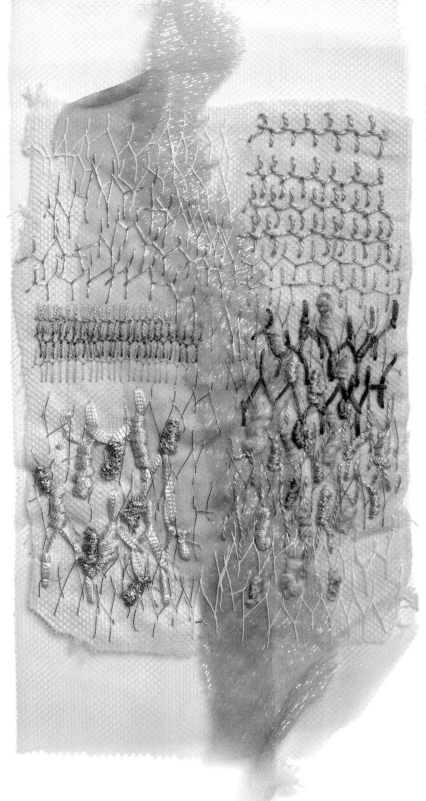

Left: In this sample piece, fly stitch was used to create a flowing line, to attach fleece fibers, and produce a random pattern.

Above: Fly stitch in different types of metallic thread was used over sheer fabric in delicate colors to create a subtle effect.

Couching

Couching is a way of attaching ornamental threads, or threads that are too chunky, to the surface of your work. Mixing different types of thread can give stunning results.

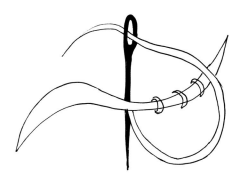

Straight Stitch

Straight stitch is a very versatile stitch and can be used to create simple line structures, overlap and create layers, or couch down other yarns and fabrics.

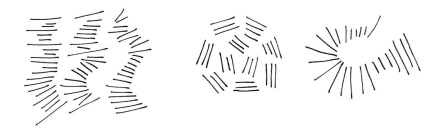

Seed Stitch

Seed stitch, which consists of many short stitches placed randomly, can be used to fill large areas and gives a delicate textured effect.

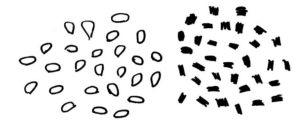

Herringbone Stitch

Herringbone stitch is a satisfying crossed stitch that can also be used to couch down cord or ribbon.

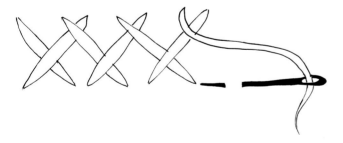

Above: In this sample, Cretan stitch has been worked in a mixture of fine threads and random stitching to create a textural background. Close formal stitching in a variety of threads created a dense, formalized area. This basic stitch forms a base, and thicker threads and tubular ribbon were wound around to create some chunky effects.

Cretan Stitch

This is another of my favorite stitches, and it can produce some wonderful textural effects.

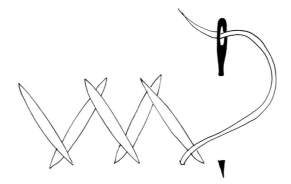

Special effects

All sorts of special effects in fabric can be created to decorate your doll.

Plaited Braids and Cords

At one time or another we have all learned to make a plait, but now it is time to explore the possibilities of this simple technique. Most of the plaited braids I use on my dolls are made from tearing strips of fabric into thin lengths. This means that I can combine different fabrics—perhaps satins and velvets, transparent nylons and polyester lining fabrics—to provide contrast. This also means that I can use the same fabrics that I have used on the dolls and keep a common color scheme.

The technique is simple; just choose your fabrics, cut them into strips and plait them together.

Here are some variations to try:
• Basic plait using a variety of fabrics
• Plaited braid with knotted tassels
• Plait a length, make a knot, leave a gap, make a knot, continue to plait
• Take a plaited braid and strip of fabric and knot randomly

A plaited braid

Right: These simple plaited braids are ideal for wrapping around figures or for using as costume detail. They are made by plaiting torn strips of fabric together.

Twisted Cords

Explore the technique of twisted cords in the same way by using strips of fabric in varying widths and textures. Plaited braids and twisted cords are very useful additions to doll making and can be used to wrap, couch down, for hair or as part of a costume.

Twisted cords are easily made:

1 Select a variety of fabric strips and yarns and knot them together at each end.

2 Loop one end over a hook and insert a pencil into the loop at the other end.

3 Keeping the thread taut, start to twist the pencil clockwise until it becomes tight.

4 Holding the central point, fold the cord in half and allow it to twist together; knot the two ends together.

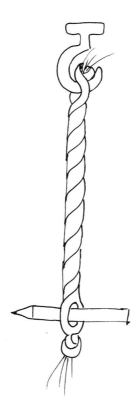

Twisted cords

Rouleau Tubes

A rouleau (*roo-loh*) or fabric tube can provide effective and exciting decoration. Experiment with different thicknesses of fabric and explore the possibilities. This is a technique that really suits the art of doll making. The rouleau tube or cord can be used to wrap around the limbs or body, adding extra shape and form to the doll. It can also be developed into wonderful costumes, headdresses and accessories. Some amazing effects can be created by wrapping and coiling the rouleau tubes and cords, and combining them with stitch will add another dimension to your work.

The basic technique of making a rouleau will enable you to make anything from a very fine delicate tube with fabrics like silk, or thick chunky tubes in something like velvet. The interest stems mainly from the choice of fabric and the way it is applied to a background. Simple stitching is all that is needed to secure a rouleau in place, but varying the threads will add extra interest.

Bias or crossway strips

To make a bias or crossway strip:

1 Fold the fabric over at 90 degrees, so that the selvedge is parallel to the weft.

2 Cut along the cross grain.

3 Cut into strips, any width you require.

To join bias strips together, lay two bias strips right sides together at a 90-degree angle and stitch together.

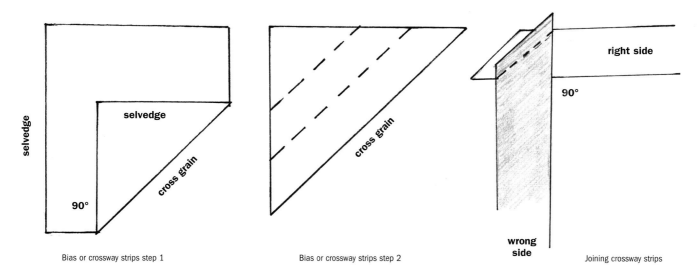

Bias or crossway strips step 1   Bias or crossway strips step 2   Joining crossway strips

Creating the rouleau tube

1 Cut a bias strip that is the finished width of the tube plus ½in (1.2cm) seam allowance.

2 Lay a piece of fine cord or string in the center of the strip and then fold the strip over.

3 Stitch across the end to secure the cord.

4 Use a zipper foot and stitch to the required width.

5 Trim the seam allowance.

6 Take hold of the cord and pull the tube inside out.

Rouleau cords

By using this method, any thickness of cord can be covered with fabric. The core can be made from materials as fine as wool or as thick as rope. Once again, experiment to find the real potential of this technique.

1 Cut a piece of cord to twice the required finished length.

2 Cut a crossway strip wide enough to cover the core plus ½in (1.2cm) seam allowance.

Creating a rouleau tube

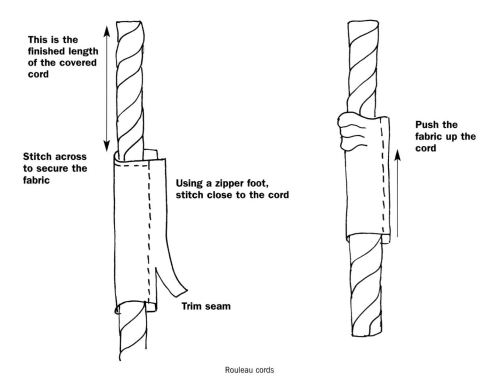

This is the finished length of the covered cord

Stitch across to secure the fabric

Using a zipper foot, stitch close to the cord

Trim seam

Push the fabric up the cord

Rouleau cords

On the next two pages are a selection of rouleau tubes and cords, including the following:

- Rouleau cord made with dyed scrim was knotted and wrapped in silver tubular braid. This rouleau has a thick rope core and is covered with a polyester brocade. The cord is knotted and stitched down with stranded cotton in buttonhole stitch.
- A fine rouleau tube made from polyester lining was stitched down with variegated floss thread and detached chain stitch.
- A wiggly rouleau cord is made from gold and plum brocade and is stitched down from the back with a running stitch.
- A thick rouleau cord covered in a rich red and gold brocade was wrapped with a tubular braid and stitched from the back with running stitch.
- The fabric on one of the rouleau cords was ruched and then randomly stitched with variegated pearl cotton in buttonhole stitch.
- A luscious rayon velvet tube was stitched down with variegated floss in fly stitch.
- This fine brocade tube was knotted and then stitched down with straight stitch.
- A rich rayon velvet cord was created in the same way as the tube above, but has achieved an entirely different effect. It is stitched in place with variegated stranded cotton.
- A scrim cord was ruched, secured with buttonhole stitch in variegated rayon floss.
- A rouleau tube was stitched down with detached chain stitch and because the thread and fabric are of a similar color, the effect is very muted.
- A simple herringbone stitch secures this satin rouleau cord.
- A velvet rouleau tube was made longer than the core, then ruched to produce a scrunchy texture.
- Two rouleau tubes were overlapped and stitched down with herringbone stitch and buttonhole stitch.
- A satin rouleau tube was stitched down with a variegated pearl cotton thread in fly stitch.

Pages 86–87: The rouleau tubes and cords described above were attached to the background fabric with buttonhole stitch, fly stitch, detached chain stitch and running stitch.

Frills and Puffs

Frills and puffs are very versatile techniques that can give volume and style to your doll. They can be used to make very effective puffed sleeves or even on legs. To make a basic puff:

Technique:

1 Cut a strip of fabric and machine stitch the short sides together.

2 Turn a narrow hem and run a gathering stitch around the top and bottom.

3 Stitch top gathers in place, leaving a gap, and stitch lower gathers in place. These puffs can be either single or grouped together.

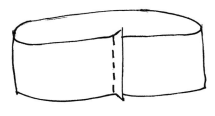

Basic puff step 1

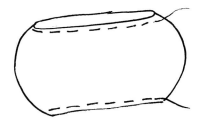

Basic puff step 2

Basic puff step 3

Flat puffs

To make a flatter, less bouncy puff, use the following technique:

1 Join a strip of fabric together at the short ends.

2 Press a narrow hem at the top and the bottom.

3 Fold the strip in half and run a gathering stitch around the top edge.

4 Pull up to fit and stitch in place.

Opposite: Puffs in a vibrant sheer fabric are used to suggest flouncy sleeves on this doll.

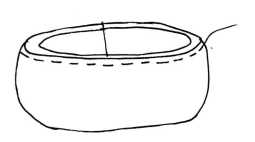

Flat puff step 3

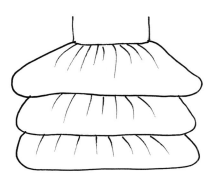

Flat puff step 4

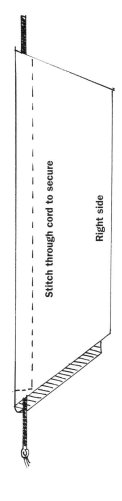

Stitch through cord to secure

Right side

Frill step 4

Frills

People tend to think of frills as things that are just stuck on the end of skirts, but this simple and versatile technique has endless possibilities that will enhance any project. They can add another dimension and a sense of glamour to any doll, not just as costume but as texture too. Different fabrics will react differently to the technique: Nylon fabric will produce a springy, bouncy frill; velvet will produce a rich, sumptuous, compact frill, and scrim (gauze-type drapery fabric) a ragged, rough frill.

1 Cut a bias strip to the required width.
2 Put a knot in one end of a fine cord, lay it in the middle of the bias strip and fold the strip in half.
3 Using a zipper foot, machine stitch close to the cord.
4 Secure one end of the cord by stitching securely and then pull the frill up to the required length.

Try experimenting with:
• Different fabrics: perhaps velvet, scrim, polyester lining, brocade or sheer nylon
• Mixing different fabrics together in the same frill
• Using two fabrics of different lengths
• Varying the width of the frill—start with a strip of fabric that is wider at one end and narrower at the other
• Using fabrics of two or three different colors together in one frill
• Combining fabrics that have different textures and finishes.

Right: These simple frills have been made from polyester lining fabric, dyed scrim, sheer nylon and velvet. The combination of different widths and fabrics creates a rich texture.

chapter three
Stuffed Cloth Dolls

Right: Transfer paints, appliqué and free-machine embroidery were used to make the fabric for this stuffed cloth doll, and the costume was made using free-machine embroidery on water-soluble fabric.

Although it is the most difficult to make of the three types of dolls covered in this book, the structure of the stuffed cloth doll is basic and therefore provides us with the opportunity to be creative with the fabric from which the doll is constructed. I often use transfer paints, appliqué, free-machine embroidery and cutwork to create fabrics with depth and texture.

If you fix the head and limbs at different angles and positions on a stuffed cloth doll, you will be able to create movement and character.

Materials and Equipment for the Basic Stuffed Cloth Doll

You will need:

- ½ yard (0.5m) calico or similar for background fabric
- Wonder Under (Bondaweb)
- ¼ yard (0.25m) 100% cotton fabric in flesh color for head and hands
- Strong thread for needle-sculpting
- Colored pencils
- Waterproof and fade-proof pens
- Acrylic spray coating
- Long darning needle
- Chenille stems
- Toy stuffing
- Water-soluble stabilizer, such as AquaFilm or Sulky Solvy: a medium-weight cold-water-soluble film (it looks like plastic). It can be free-machine stitched and then dissolved in cold water, leaving the stitching unsupported. It can also be used to stabilize fine fabric while it is being stitched into. Guliette and Verona, made in England, are also suitable medium-weight water-soluble films that can be used.
- Sheer nylon fabrics and other synthetic fabrics that will melt with a soldering iron. Experiment with a variety of fabrics before you start.
- Protective mask or respirator: some synthetic fabrics emit fumes that may irritate the eyes and throat.
- Ballpoint or waterproof artist's pen for drawing onto the water-soluble stabilizer.
- Embroidery hoop
- Sewing-machine threads that resist heat: Sylko, Madeira metallic, etc. If you are unsure which to use, always test them first.
- A piece of glass (cover the edges with masking tape) or a nonstick cooking liner available from household stores: These are to prevent the heat from the soldering iron penetrating the surface underneath.
- Soldering iron with a fine tip: The most suitable kind can be bought from a craft supplier, rather than from a do-it-yourself store or hardware store.

Opposite: Elaborate fabrics can be added to the simple stuffed cloth doll shape to create life and movement. The skirt and bodice of this costume was made using cutwork with a soldering iron (see page 115). The underskirt was made using water-soluble film and free-machine embroidery.

Using transfer paints and dyes

Transfer paints and dyes are simple, versatile, and effective materials for transforming plain fabrics into fabulous textiles. They are designed specifically to be used on synthetic fabrics and bold, vibrant, textured, as well as soft, muted patterns, can be achieved. Exciting surfaces with real depth can also be created by overprinting and layering. Experiment with these exciting techniques and you will produce some fabulous fabrics for your cloth doll.

For transfer-painting techniques, you will need:
- Protective cover for your ironing board
- An old iron: I always keep an old iron to use for craft work to prevent cross-contamination.
- Parchment paper
- Transfer paints or dyes
- Palette or old plate for mixing paints on
- Jam jar and water
- Paper: It is best not to use too thick a paper as the heat will not penetrate effectively; also avoid using paper that is too absorbent as it will soak up the paint. I find photocopy paper and pattern paper both work well.
- Fabric: Most synthetic fabrics are suitable but experiment with different textures and weights—polyester lining, satin, sheer nylon, lace and net, etc. (It is not necessary to use only white fabric; try pale or mid-tone colors for the background, as they can add a richness to your finished fabric.)
- Equipment for making marks, texture and pattern
- Paintbrushes in various shapes and sizes
- Household or natural sponges and sponge brushes
- Stencils: commercial or homemade
- Stamps: commercial or homemade
- Plastic wrap (Saran Wrap)
- Leaves and flowers

Transfer Paints and Dyes

Transfer paints are a little thicker than the dyes, and can be mixed and applied like most paint mediums. They can also be diluted with water to produce pale colors.

Transfer dyes (sometimes called disperse dyes) are a powder that is mixed with water, producing a thinner solution than the paints. These can also be mixed together to produce a wide range of colors.

You can test out transfer paints and dyes on paper, but the end result when you use them on fabric can look completely different. On fabric, the colors tend to be a lot brighter. By making and keeping a color chart on fabric to show the "true" colors, you will be able to make better choices about the colors you want to use on future projects. This chart can include mixed colors as well as the pure dyes. It is not always necessary to use a white background for your color chart. If you prefer to work on pale or mid-toned color fabrics, why not use that fabric for your color chart to ensure accuracy?

Here is how I create my color charts:
1 Paint each color onto a piece of paper and label.
2 Iron onto a piece of synthetic fabric.
3 Staple the paper and fabric together matching the corresponding colors.

You may also want to keep a color reference notebook when you are mixing colors. I always think I will remember which colors I have used but I never do. A color notebook is also very necessary if you want to produce a large area of pattern or repeat something at a later date.

Above: This chart shows the colors of the transfer paints on paper (left) and the true colors on fabric (right).

Applying the paint

The paint can be applied in a variety of different ways, so indulge in some experimentation, but be warned: It can become compulsive.

• Random stippling effects can be achieved by using a damp sponge, stencil brush or scrunched-up paper.

• Found objects, commercial stamps, and homemade stamps can create patterns. Leaves and flowers can also be used to make delicate floral patterns. Apply the paint to the object and stamp onto the paper.

• Commercial and homemade stencils will produce strong, bold patterns, and lace or plastic doilies will give a delicate, lacy finish.

• Brushes in different shapes and sizes will make a huge variety of interesting marks; sponge brushes are also very effective.

• Plastic wrap (Saran Wrap), scrunched up on wet paint and left to dry will produce a web-like effect.

Below and opposite: Turquoise, yellow and red paint was splodged onto dampened paper (below), and the colors were then merged together. It was then printed onto a pale blue polyester fabric (opposite).

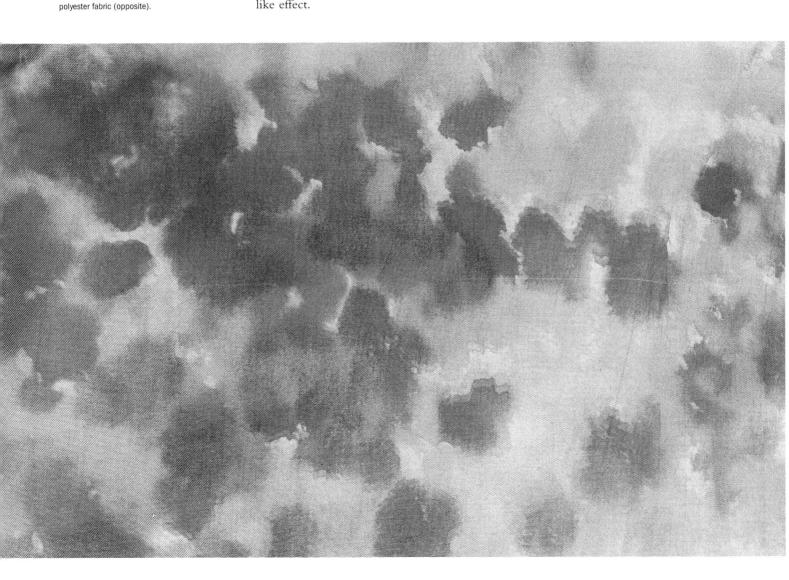

Creating Layers and Depth

• If you use several colors on your brush, sponge or stamp, you will develop interesting variegated finishes.

• Sponge, stamp or stipple with one color and then overprint with another color to create layers and depth. This technique is also very effective when used with stamps.

• Paint a piece of paper, cut out a motif and then use the motif to print with.

Method

1 Apply the paint to the paper and leave to dry thoroughly.

2 Iron out any creases in your fabric and place the printed paper, paint side down, on top. Cover with parchment paper and iron.

TIP Synthetic fabric should be ironed with a cool/medium iron and transfer paints need a hot iron, so it is necessary to cover the fabric with parchment paper to protect the fabric before applying the iron.

3 Move the iron slowly over the parchment paper until the print has transferred onto the fabric. This may take longer than you think, so be patient. It is possible to use the print more than once but each successive print will be paler.

TIP When making fabric for a doll, always make sure you have enough fabric made from the first print to make both sides of your pattern. Alternatively you could make two prints, one for the front and one for the back.

Opposite: A sponge brush was dipped in green transfer paint and a series of radiating lines were sponged onto the paper. The same process was done with purple paint. This was then printed onto an oyster-colored polyester lining.

Above: Watery turquoise, pink and yellow paint was splodged onto some paper and a piece of plastic wrap was scrunched up on top and left to dry. When the plastic wrap was removed, this beautifully textured paper was left behind. It was then printed onto pale green polyester satin.

Opposite: A commercial stencil was used on this piece. Turquoise, orange, yellow, and red dyes were used and the stencil was used several times to create a pattern with depth. It was then printed onto a gold and blue shot-polyester (iridescent) lining fabric.

Below: A grid pattern in yellow and purple was painted onto the paper with a paintbrush, and it was then printed onto a pale green polyester-lining fabric.

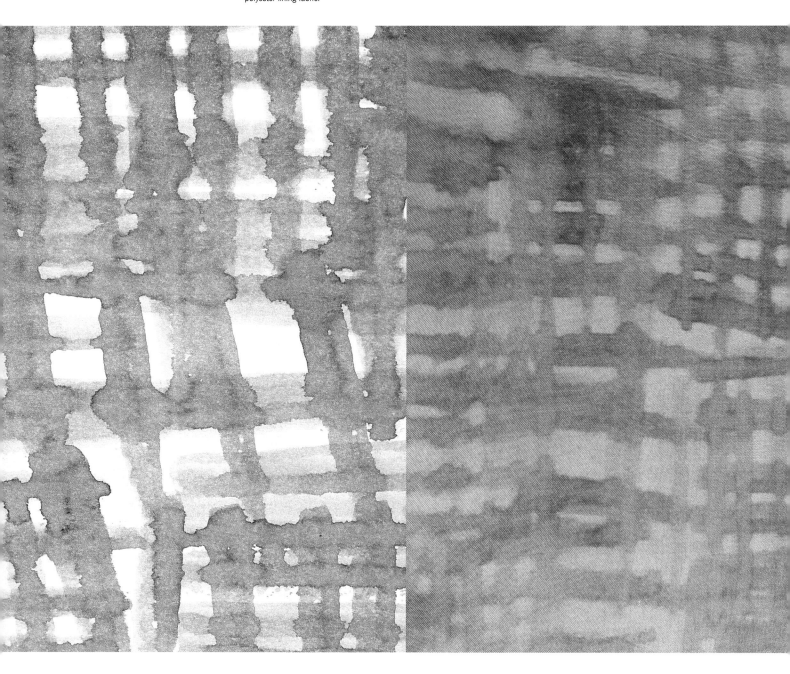

Appliqué using Wonder Under

Once you have printed your fabric, extra interest, depth, and decoration can be added with appliqué and stitch. This is a good technique for adding depth and texture to your fabric, meaning that you can create layers to provide a focus. Many different fabrics can be used: Solid fabrics will produce bold, strong shapes and sheer fabrics will give shadowy, translucent effects. The background on this sample fabric has been created using transfer paints. The motifs, made from polyester-lining fabric in a solid color, provide a focus, while the sheer nylon fabric gives an illusion of depth.

Once a background fabric has been created, it is possible to make it even richer by adding texture with stitch. The transfer painting and appliqué techniques add a depth to any fabric, but it is the stitching that really adds texture.

Below: Motifs cut out in a polyester lining fabric were applied to a transfer-painted background, using the Bondaweb technique.

You need to prepare only small amounts of fabric for your appliqué motifs.
1 Cut a piece of fabric and Wonder Under (Bondaweb) the same size.
2 Place the Wonder Under, rough side down, onto the fabric, and iron with
   a medium-to-hot iron.
3 Either draw your motif onto the paper side of the Wonder Under
   or use a template to draw around.
4 Cut the motif out and peel the paper away.
5 Place the motif (fabric side facing up) onto the
   background and iron in place. You need a
   medium-to-hot iron to make the motif secure,
   so if you are using a fine or synthetic
   fabric, cover it with parchment paper
   to protect it.

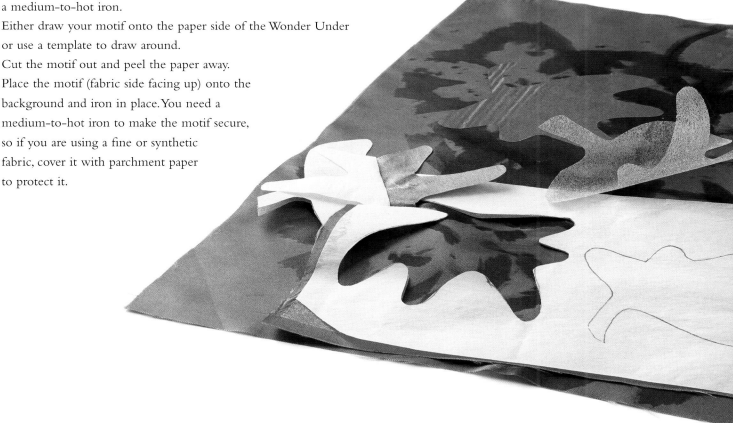

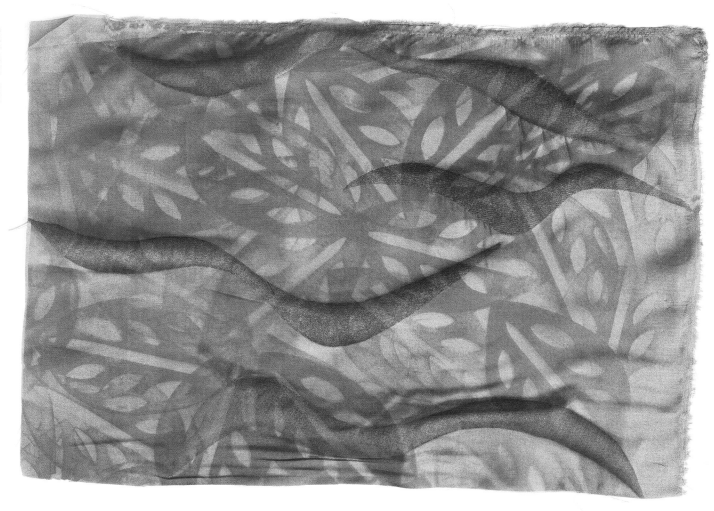

Above: A piece of polyester lining fabric was stamped with red transfer paints.

Experiment with different fabrics—perhaps sheer nylon, synthetic lining or silks. Each different fabric will bring a different quality to your work.

Free-machine embroidery will provide the fabric for your doll with an added richness and depth. Either use a random all-over stitch to blend the printing and appliqué together or accentuate the motif or pattern by outlining with stitch. Consider the thread you will use—shiny, matte, metallic—as this will also give an added texture to your work.

In the piece shown above and right, red transfer paint and a commercial stamp were used to stamp this design onto paper, which was then ironed onto a gold polyester lining. Free-machine embroidery was then used to blend the background together and to add texture, leaving the appliqué shapes to stand out.

Below: Appliqué shapes were added and the whole piece was blended together with free-machine stitching.

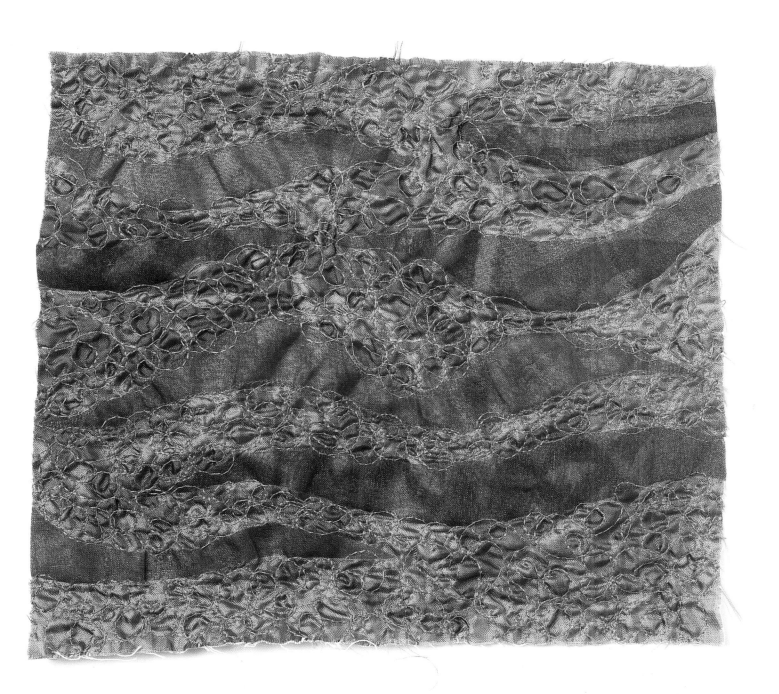

Below: Transfer paints were painted onto leaves and these were then pressed onto the paper. The paper was then ironed onto green polyester lining fabric. A variegated rayon thread and free-machine stitching were used to outline the veins of the leaf.

Above: A commercial stamp was used to apply the transfer paint to the paper. Green, red, and yellow were used on top of each other to create depth. The paper was then ironed onto a gold polyester lining and some sheer nylon appliquéd motifs were added. The appliqué motifs were left unstitched while free-machine embroidery in gold rayon thread was used to blend the background together.

Opposite: Leaves were painted and printed onto paper in subtle tones. The print was then transferred onto pale brown fabric, and free-machine embroidery was used to give the design further embellishment.

Making the stuffed cloth doll

Preparing the Fabric for the Doll

Many lightweight synthetic fabrics are not substantial enough to hold their shape or withstand stuffing, so it is advisable to back them with a firmer fabric such as calico.

Make sure that you create enough fabric for both sides of the pattern. Be generous; it is always better to have too much, rather than not enough.

1 Lay your printed and appliquéd fabric onto a piece of calico that is about 1½in (3.7cm) bigger.
2 Stretch the fabric taut in an embroidery hoop and enhance with free-machine embroidery.

You now have a piece of decorative fabric with which to make your doll.

Most of the techniques for making up the doll have already been covered, so once you have made your fabric just follow the instructions on the pages shown:

• General pattern and construction methods [page 10]
• Making and needle-sculpting the head [page 66–71]
• Drawing the face [page 36]
• Attaching the head [page 44]
• Attaching the arms [page 44]
• Making hands with fingers [page 62]

Attaching the Hands to the Arms

1 Make the arms, leaving both the top and bottom open, and turn a small hem at the wrist.
2 Push the wrist of the hand well up inside the arm and stitch together around the wrist.
3 Take small pieces of stuffing and carefully stuff around the chenille stems until you have a firm, smooth wrist. Stuff the rest of the arm.

Attaching the Legs

Before attaching the legs, try placing the limbs in different positions to see how much movement you can achieve. It is surprising what you can do with these simple shapes. You may find it easier to use long pins to hold the legs securely.

Once you are happy with the position, use a long darning needle and strong thread and ladder-stitch all the way around.

Right: This doll's costume was created by machine stitching on sheer nylon fabric and then cutting out the design with a soldering iron. A spectacular headdress was made using the same fabric.

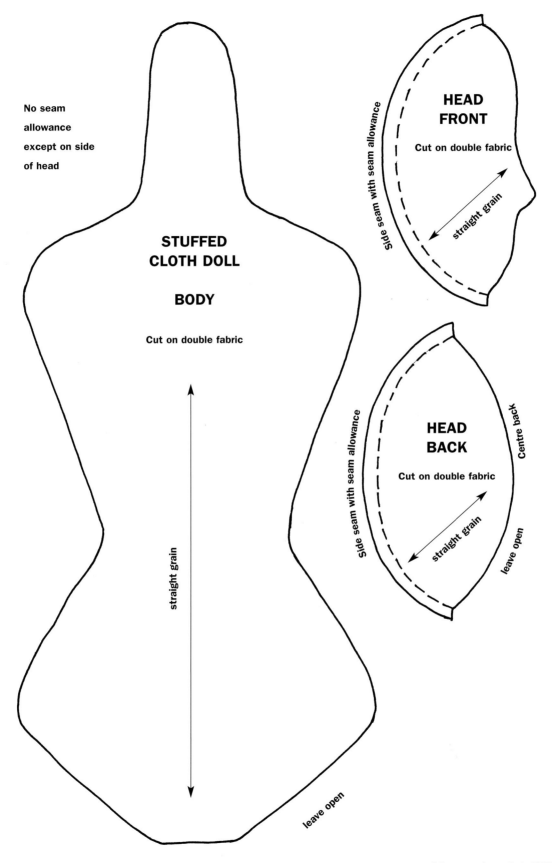

**No seam
allowance
except on side
of head**

**STUFFED
CLOTH DOLL**

BODY

Cut on double fabric

straight grain

leave open

**HEAD
FRONT**

Cut on double fabric

Side seam with seam allowance

straight grain

**HEAD
BACK**

Cut on double fabric

Side seam with seam allowance

Centre back

straight grain

leave open

Enlarge on a photocopier by 115%

Stuffed cloth doll patterns

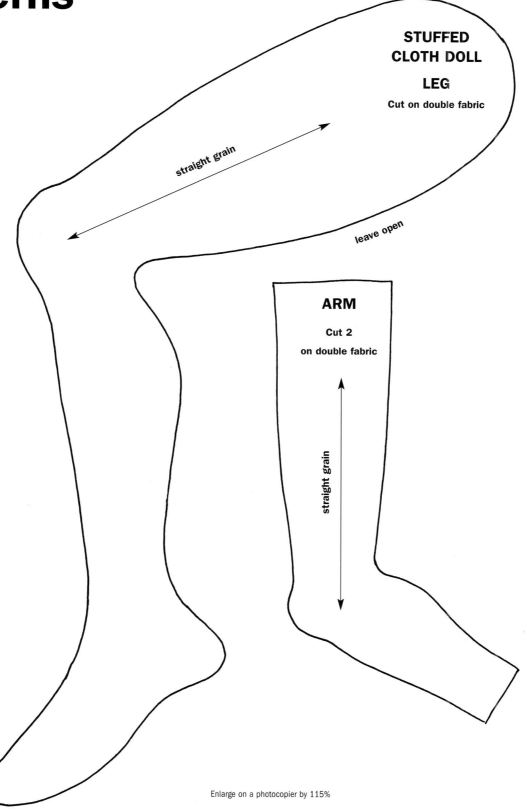

**STUFFED
CLOTH DOLL**

LEG

Cut on double fabric

straight grain

leave open

ARM

Cut 2

on double fabric

straight grain

Enlarge on a photocopier by 115%

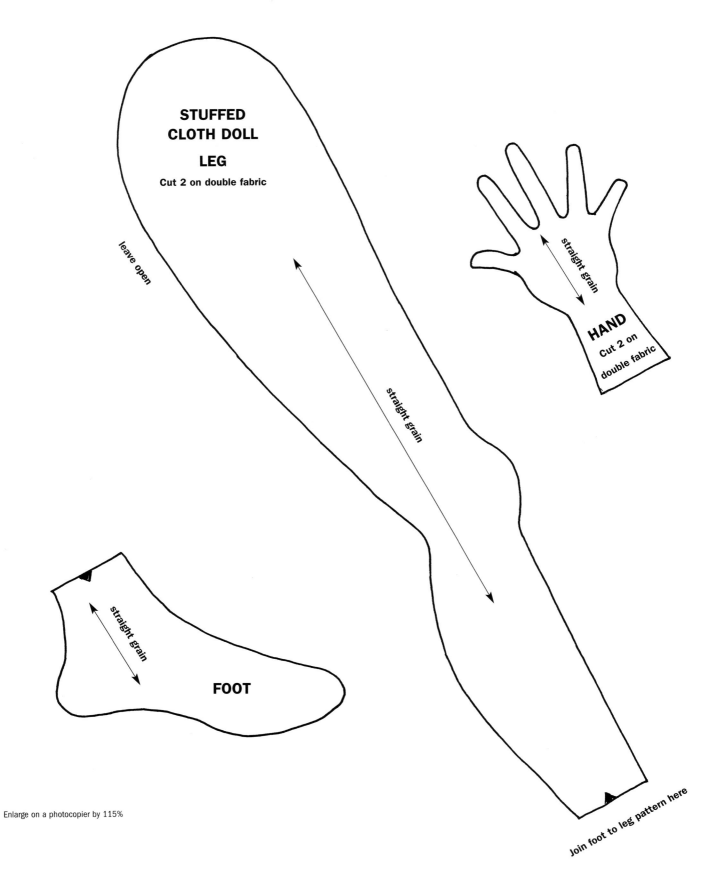

STUFFED CLOTH DOLL

LEG

Cut 2 on double fabric

leave open

straight grain

HAND

Cut 2 on double fabric

straight grain

straight grain

FOOT

Join foot to leg pattern here

Enlarge on a photocopier by 115%

Creating cutwork fabric using a soldering iron

Because this exciting technique is so versatile it presents many possibilities for costuming a doll. One of the best things about this technique is the fact that you can make a piece of fabric any shape or size you want. Decide what finished shape you want and then create your design within it. This has some distinct advantages when you are dealing with dolls' costumes as you can work to any scale you want. It is also possible to make your finished design fit into any shape, create a curvy or asymmetrical hemline, or fit a design into a wing or fan shape, and it is an excellent technique for making individual motifs and decorations, such as leaves.

First start by choosing a design that suits the theme of your doll. It may be abstract or floral or it may have a fantasy inspiration. Whatever you choose, it is worth spending a little time developing your design. If you do not wish to create your own design, there are many inspirational copyright-free design books on the market. These books allow you to use their designs without infringing copyright laws.

It is possible to make single motifs or large areas of "fabric" with this technique. There are only a few rules to consider:

- Keep your design within the scale of your doll.
- If you making a large piece of "fabric," make sure that all parts of the design connect together, otherwise your "fabric" will fall apart.

Right: Polyester lining fabric was cut into rough strips with a hot soldering iron, then laid between two pieces of water-soluble film. The strips were connected with free-machine embroidery. The motif at the top was made in polyester lining fabric and stitched in variegated metallic thread.

Step 2

Step 6

Method

1 Draw out the design on paper and outline in black pen.

2 Place a piece of water-soluble stabilizer on top of the design and secure it with masking tape to keep it flat.

> **TIP** The fabric and water-soluble stabilizer should be bigger than the finished design so that there is enough to stretch it in an embroidery hoop.

3 Trace the design onto the water-soluble stabilizer using a ballpoint or waterproof pen.

4 Place the water-soluble stabilizer on top of two pieces of sheer nylon fabric. You can use two different colors to create more interesting effects.

5 Carefully stretch the water-soluble stabilizer and nylon in an embroidery hoop.

6 Follow the line of the design and free-machine stitch at least two rows of stitching around the design.

7 Carefully cut away any excess water-soluble stabilizer and submerge the piece in cold water until the film has dissolved.

8 Dry the piece of work thoroughly.

9 Lay the work on a piece of glass or sheet of non-stick liner and, using a hot soldering iron, cut out all the required areas. Use a mask or respirator to protect yourself from any fumes.

Top left: Preparing the fabric for the cutwork technique. The design is traced onto Aquafilm, then it is stretched on top of two pieces of sheer nylon fabric in an embroidery hoop, and free-machine stitched around the design.

Middle left: Once the Aquafilm has dissolved away, motifs are cut out using a soldering iron.

Bottom left: This interlocking design was stitched in metallic thread before the Aquafilm was dissolved away. When the piece was dry, the excess fabric was cut away with a hot soldering iron.

Cutting motifs

Cutting out sheer nylon fabric and slippery lining with scissors can be quite tricky, but if you use a soldering iron you can produce intricate designs more easily.

1 Draw out your shapes on paper and then trace onto freezer paper.

2 Cut out the shapes and iron (with the shiny side down) onto the fabric.

3 Use a hot soldering iron to cut around the freezer paper. Peel the paper away, revealing the intricate shapes.

4 Lay the motifs between two pieces of water-soluble stabilizer and pin in place.

5 Carefully stretch this sandwich in an embroidery hoop and free-machine stitch in between the motifs, connecting them together.

6 Dissolve in the usual way.

Above: Random shapes were cut out of polyester lining fabric with a soldering iron, sandwiched between two pieces of water-soluble film and linked together with free-machine stitching.

Left: This fabric was created by cutting random shapes of sheer nylon fabric with a soldering iron, sandwiching them between water-soluble film and linking them together with free-machine stitching.

Above: Synthetic fabrics can be cut into intricate shapes with a hot soldering iron. Polyester lining and sheer nylon fabrics both work well for this technique.

Creating fabrics with water-soluble film

Water-soluble film is the ideal product for making soft lacy fabrics for costuming dolls. Beautiful weblike fabrics can be created, motifs can be suspended within the web and threads incorporated in the structures.

Once again, if you explore and experiment with the technique, you will produce some wonderful and exciting fabrics for your doll.

Method

1 Stretch the film taut in an embroidery hoop. If you feel that the film you are using is too thin, use it doubled.

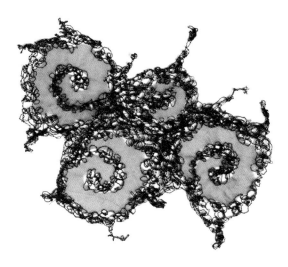

Above: Sheer nylon motifs were cut out using a soldering iron, sandwiched between two pieces of water-soluble film (above) and linked together with free-machine stitching to form a soft, lacy fabric (right).

Pages 120–121: This piece of fabric was made by sandwiching sparkly Christmas fibers between two pieces of water-soluble film and stitching together with blue thread. A pattern was then stitched on top in gold metallic thread.

2 Set your machine for free-machine embroidery and create a grid. Once this is done, you can add more decorative stitching on top.
3 Cut away any excess film and submerge the piece in cold water until all the film has been dissolved.

• The bobbin thread will show through in this technique, so consider this when choosing your thread.
• It is important to provide a background grid to support the stitching. If you do not have this supporting background, the stitching won't hang together. It doesn't matter what form the grid takes, so long as it is interlocking. Once the grid is complete, more stitching can be done on top.

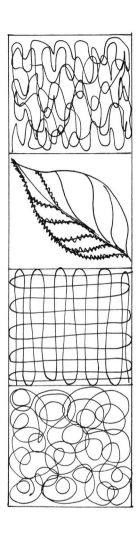

- If you want your piece to be soft like a piece of fabric, change the water and rinse several times.
- If you want to mold your fabric into a shape, stop rinsing at the jelly stage and gently press over a mold such as a bowl or a spoon and leave to dry.
- To add richness to a basic web of stitching it is possible to add snippets of fabric or fibers.

Above left: Some pattern suggestions for free-machine stitching your fabric.

Above right: Soft, lacy fabric created using the water-soluble film technique can look great draped around a doll to suggest a delicate skirt.

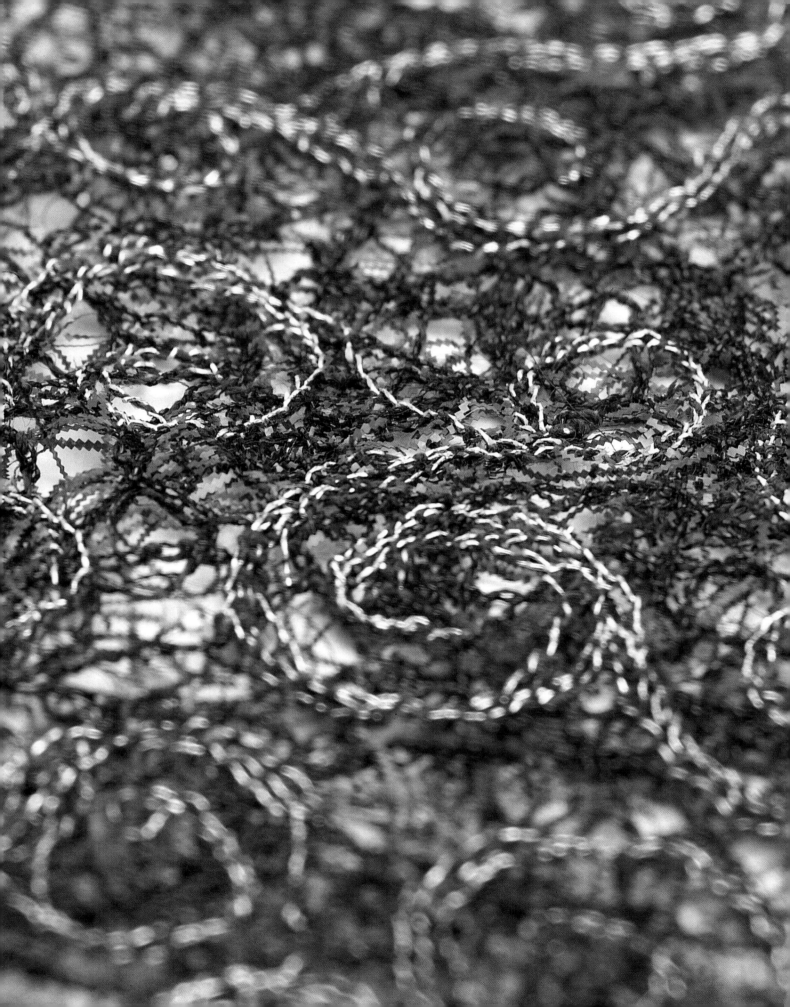

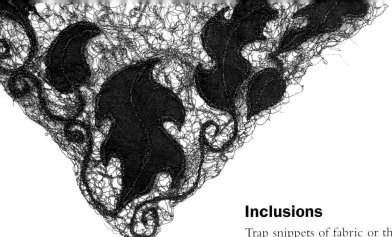

Inclusions

Trap snippets of fabric or thread in between two layers of water-soluble stabilizer, stretch in an embroidery hoop and free-machine stitch over the top. Dissolve in the usual way.

Adding Appliqué Motifs

Once you have created a background grid or web, it is possible to add appliqué and stitch to enrich your fabric.

1 Stretch water-soluble stabilizer in a hoop and free-machine stitch a background grid or web.
2 Iron some Wonder Under onto the back of the fabric that you are going to use for your appliqué, cut out a motif, and peel the paper away.
3 Lay the motif onto the background web, fabric side facing up, cover with parchment paper, and iron into place.
4 Free-machine stitch two rows of straight stitch around the motif.
5 If you wish to add thicker lines, set your machine to zigzag and free-machine stitch to complete your decoration.
6 Dissolve in the usual way.

Above: For this fabric, the background was created using metallic bronze threads and free-machine embroidery. Leaf shapes were appliquéd on top and edged in bronze metallic thread.

Above right and right: This motif was created in spotted synthetic fabric and linked together with free-machine embroidery. It was then appliquéd to a colorful background fabric.

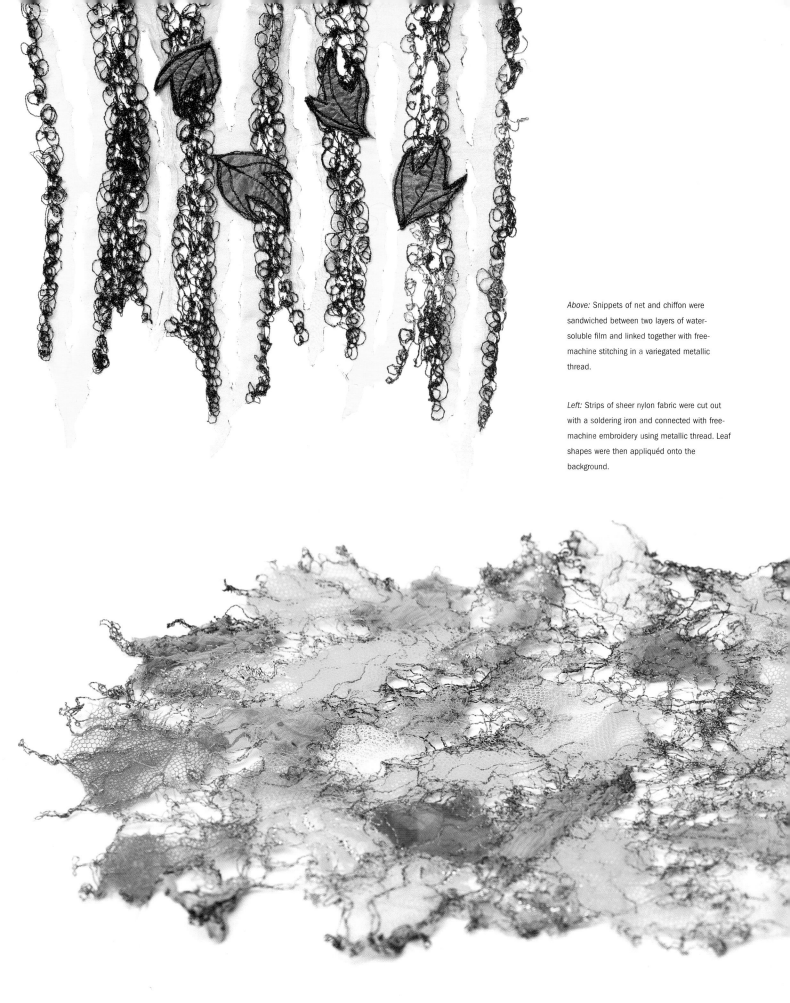

Above: Snippets of net and chiffon were sandwiched between two layers of water-soluble film and linked together with free-machine stitching in a variegated metallic thread.

Left: Strips of sheer nylon fabric were cut out with a soldering iron and connected with free-machine embroidery using metallic thread. Leaf shapes were then appliquéd onto the background.

Left: Dyed Wensleydale fleece was used to create this bouncy, curly hairstyle.

Hairstyles and headdresses

Every doll needs its crowning glory and needle felting is a quick-and-easy way to achieve this. Each character will need a different hairdo, so look through fashion and hair magazines for ideas. I keep a folder of magazine clippings, which I find invaluable as a source of inspiration.

Needle-felting Hair

This technique will enable you to attach a variety of fibers to the head without any stitching. The fibers are stabbed into the head with a felting needle. This needle has a double-barbed tip that pushes the fibers into the head and secures them in place.

Most wool fibers will work with this method:
- Merino wool tops are combed woolen fibers that come in a huge variety of colors.
- Wool fleece is the fleece cut from a sheep's back and is not combed or spun. When washed and dyed it makes wonderful hair. Wensleydale fleece has curly fibers and Blue-faced Leicester fleece has crinkly fibers.
- Woolen yarns with soft fibers work best as the needle can penetrate them more easily.
- Silk fibers also can be used, but they are denser and require a little more work to secure them.

Before you start using the felting needle, arrange the fibers on the head and try out a few styles. When you are happy with your arrangement, hold the felting needle at a slight angle and stab repeatedly into the fibers and head. This process will secure the fibers. If you don't like your first attempt, pull the fibers out and start again.

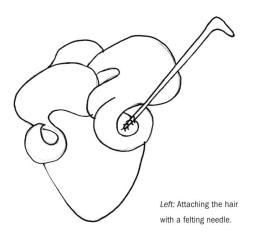

Left: Attaching the hair with a felting needle.

Top right: This wild hair was created by cutting dyed woolen yarn into lengths and needle-felting it into the head.

Right: Merino wool tops were twisted and piled up to create this bouffant hairdo. Curly Wensleydale fleece in a matching color was attached to the sides to add a bit of "spring."

Headddresses

Headdresses can be made using
many of the techniques that have
been discussed earlier in the book,
for example, cutwork fabrics and
crossway waves. Here are some
examples.

Above: An interlocking design was created for
this headdress before it was stitched in metallic
thread and cut away with a soldering iron.

Right: A variety of fabric were used in this
stitched crossway wave structure to create a
fluid and exotic headdress.

Useful Suppliers

Blick Art Materials
PO Box 1267
Galesburg, IL 61402-1267
(800) 933-2542
www.dickblick.com
(Waterproof pens and other art supplies)

Dharma Trading Company
1604 Fourth St.
San Rafael, CA 94901
(800) 542-5227 or (415) 456-7657
www.dharmatrading.com
(Dyes, fabric paints, fabrics)

Fabrics to Dye For
PO Box 803
Blanco, TX 78606
(888) 322-1319 or (830) 833-5300
www.fabricstodyefor.com
(Quilting, sewing, surface design, and knitting supplies)

Forest Hollow Studio
9000 Westwood
Kirtland, OH 44094
www.foresthollowstudio.com
(Doll-making supplies, tools, dyed fleece)

Erica's Craft & Sewing Center
1320 North Ironwood Dr.
South Bend, IN 46615
(888) 837-4227
www.ericas.com
(Doll-making supplies, Guliette and Verona embroidery stabilizers)

Impress Me
17116 Escalon Dr.
Encino, CA 91436-4030
(818) 788-6730
www.impressmenow.com
(Stamping supplies)

Meinke Toy
www.meinketoy.com
(Carries surface design products more common in the U.K.)

***PieceWork* magazine**
www.interweave.com/needle/
needlework_resources
(Resource links for needlework)

PRO Chemical & Dye
PO Box 14
Somerset, MA 02726
(800) 228-9393 or (508 676-3838)
(Disperse dyes, fabric paints)

***Quilting Arts* magazine**
23 Gleasondale Rd.
Stow, MA 01775
(866) 698-6989
www.quiltingarts.com
(Sewing and surface design supplies)

Soft Expressions
1230 North Jefferson St., Ste. M
Anaheim, CA 92807
http://softexpressions.com
(Quilting supplies, fabric paints, transfer supplies, threads)

***Spin-Off* magazine**
www.interweave.com/spin/resources
(Resource links for wool fibers)

Wet Paint Inc.
1684 Grand Ave.
St. Paul, MN 55105
(651) 698-6431
www.wetpaintart.com
(art supplies)

Further Reading

Fiberarts magazine
PieceWork magazine
(www.interweave.com)

Campbell-Harding, Valerie, and Maggie Grey. *Layers of Stitch*. London: Batsford, 2001.

Campbell-Harding, Valerie, and Maggie Grey. *Machine Embroidery: Stitched Patterns*. London: Batsford, 1997.

Culea, Patti Medaris. *Creative Cloth Doll Making: New Approaches Using Fibres, Beads, Dyes and Other Exciting Techniques.* London: Apple Press, 2003.

Howard, Constance. *The Constance Howard Book of Stitches*. London: Batsford, 2005.

Oroyan, Susanna. *Anatomy of a Doll*. Concord: C&T Publishing Inc., 1997.

Oroyan, Susanna. *Designing the Doll: From Concept to Construction*. Concord: C&T Publishing Inc., 1999.

Owen, Barbara. *Creating Faces: Needle Sculpting from the Beginning*. Designs by BJ, city of publication and date unknown.

Index